5
INGREDIENTS

CAKES &
DESSERTS

An Hachette UK Company
www.hachette.co.uk

First published in Great Britain in 2015 by
Hamlyn, a division of Octopus Publishing Group Ltd
Endeavour House
189 Shaftesbury Avenue
London WC2H 8JY

Some of the recipes in this book have previously appeared in other books published
by Hamlyn.

ISBN 978 0 60062 911 5

A CIP catalogue record for this book is available from the British Library

Printed and bound in China

10 9 8 7 6 5 4 3 2

Commissioning Editor Eleanor Maxfield
Senior Editor Sybella Stephens
Designers Jeremy Tilston, Jaz Bahra & Eoghan O'Brien
Production Controller Allison Gonsalves

Standard level spoon measurement are used in all recipes.
1 tablespoon = one 15 ml spoon
1 teaspoon = one 5 ml spoon

Both imperial and metric measurements have been given in all recipes.
Use one set of measurements only and not a mixture of both.

Eggs should be medium unless otherwise stated. The Department of Health advises
that eggs should not be consumed raw. This book contains dishes made with raw or
lightly cooked eggs. It is prudent for more vulnerable people such as pregnant and
nursing mothers, invalids, the elderly, babies and young children to avoid uncooked
or lightly cooked dishes made with eggs. Once prepared these dishes should be
kept refrigerated and used promptly.

Milk should be full-fat unless otherwise stated.

Ovens should be preheated to the specific temperature – if using a fan-assisted
oven, follow manufacturer's instructions for adjusting the time and the temperature.

All microwave information is based on a 650 watt oven. Follow manufacturer's
instructions for an oven with a different wattage.

This book includes dishes made with nuts and nut derivatives. It is advisable for
customers with known allergic reactions to nuts and nut derivatives and those
who may be potentially vulnerable to these allergies, such as pregnant and nursing
mothers, invalids, the elderly, babies and children, to avoid dishes made with nuts
and nut oils. It is also prudent to check the labels of pre-prepared Ingredients for
the possible inclusion of nut derivatives.

JUST 5 INGREDIENTS

CAKES & DESSERTS

MAKE LIFE SIMPLE WITH MORE THAN 100 RECIPES USING 5 INGREDIENTS OR FEWER

hamlyn

CONTENTS

INTRODUCTION   6

WEEKLY PLANNER   10

5 FOR...   14

FRUITY   20

CHOCOLATE   62

DECADENT TREATS   88

FAMILY FAVOURITES   120

MINI BITES   156

INDEX   190

PICTURE CREDITS   192

INTRODUCTION

The recipes in this book have been chosen not only for their simplicity and great flavours, but also because they use just five or fewer main ingredients.

Applying a five-ingredient approach to cooking will help you create a repertoire of quick, easy adaptable dishes that are not only cheap and tasty but that also require little shopping and preparation. You will learn to master some basic recipes in record time and learn to appreciate that cooking for yourself is a satisfying and empowering process.

This approach will make your life easier in three ways. First, because the recipes are straightforward there is less fiddly preparation, which will save you time. Second, you will find that shopping is simpler. How long do you really want to wander around a supermarket searching for something to cook? And third, it will save you money. The five-ingredient approach will mean that you don't have a fridge full of half-used packets of strange Ingredients, left over from previous recipes that you will never use again.

Unlike other five-ingredient cookbooks, you won't have hundreds of hidden added extras to stock up on.

This series requires you to remember a few storecupboard

extras only – simple, easy to remember basics you will no doubt already have to hand.

Start by stocking up on your storecupboard items (see page 11 and 13). Make sure you have at least some of them at home at all times so that you know you are just five ingredients away from a decent dessert.

Next, choose a recipe that suits the time you have to cook, your energy levels and your mood. Check what storecupboard ingredients you will need on the list. The five key ingredients you will need to buy and complete the dish are clearly numbered.

One of the best ways to eat cheaply is to avoid costly processed foods. Instead, buy basic ingredients such as vegetables, rice, pasta, fish and chicken, and build your meals around these. You should also try to avoid waste and not spend money on food you don't eat and that has to be thrown away. Buy food that lasts and plan around the lifetime dates of foods. If you have a freezer, freeze the leftovers for another day.

Plan your meals for the week so you need to go shopping only once a week. When you get into the habit of doing this the ingredients for each meal will be waiting when you need them.

Buy in bulk to get the best prices. Make time to shop around and compare prices in the nearest supermarket, online, your local shops and on market stalls to see which is cheapest. Stick to buying fruit and vegetables that are in season. Not only will they be better value than exotic produce flown in from abroad but you will be reducing your food miles. Finally, don't even think about spending precious cash on a supermarket's special

offer unless it is something you will actually use. Three tins of pilchards in mustard sauce for the price of one is good value only if you are going to eat them.

Not many people can resist a cake or a dessert. A good one will cheer you up after a bad day at work, banish the blues and make a grand finale to a special meal or a welcome alternative gift for a friend.

Of all the different types of cooking, baking cakes continues to thrive as the one we love most. It's a fun, enjoyable way to spend a bit of time and appeals to all ages. It's not difficult to see why baking has such enduring popularity - not only does it produce comfort food at its best (who doesn't like a wedge of chocolate cake?), it's also inexpensive and doesn't require advanced culinary knowledge or a kitchen packed with special equipment.

The secret of the perfect dessert is to ensure you have chosen the right one as part of a meal. So if you have a heavy main course, choose a light, fruity pudding, or a pastry or chocolate dessert can follow a lighter main course. The time of year will influence your choice, so in winter, you might be craving a warming comfort pudding whereas in summer something fruitier will likely take your fancy. Make use of fruits when they are in season and plentiful, as they will taste so much better, even when served simply with a scoop of ice cream or griddled with a sprinkling of sugar.

Short of time? You can cheat and use shop-bought puff or sweet shortcrust pastry. These days, our busy schedules mean a homemade pudding or cake is a treat rather than an everyday occurrence, but when you do have the time to make one, it is not only immensely rewarding but also a great way to unwind.

WEEKLY PLANNER

SOMETHING TO CELEBRATE

MONDAY
Caramel Ice Cream Cake (see page 98)

TUESDAY
Classic Lemon Tart (see page 102)

WEDNESDAY
Easy Chocolate Fudge Cake (see page 64)

THURSDAY
Strawberry Rosé Jelly & Syllabub (see page 96)

FRIDAY
Chocolate & Raspberry Soufflés (see page 76)

SATURDAY
Nectarine Brûlée (see page 92)

STORECUPBOARD

The only extras you will need!

1 Sugars
2 Flours
3 Oils & vinegars
4 Baking powder
5 Bicarbonate of soda
6 Salt
7 Lemons & lemon juice

SUNDAY
Chocolate Millefeuilles (see page 108)

SHOPPING LIST:

Fruit & nuts
- 1 lemon
- 150 ml (¼ pint) lemon juice
- 250 g (8 oz) small strawberries
- 500 g (1 lb) nectarines
- 250 g (8½ oz) raspberries
- chopped nuts, for decoration

Dairy
- 250 g (8 oz) mascarpone cheese
- 350 ml (12 fl oz) soured cream
- 700 ml (1 pint 3 fl oz) double cream
- 2 tablespoons single cream
- 200 ml (7 fl oz) single cream
- 1 litre (1¾ pints) good-quality vanilla ice cream
- 275 g (9 oz) butter
- nutmeg
- 11 eggs
- 1 kg 125 g (2 lb 5 oz) dark chocolate
- 200 g (7 oz) milk chocolate

Bottles, tins & packets
- 275 g (9 oz) self-raising flour
- 350 g (12 oz) caster sugar
- 125 g (4 oz) soft light brown sugar
- icing sugar
- 250 g (8 oz) digestive biscuits
- 200 g (7 oz) soft butterscotch fudge
- 450 g (14½ oz) chilled ready-made sweet shortcrust pastry
- 1 sachet powdered gelatine
- vanilla extract
- rosé wine
- orange liqueur

WEEKLY PLANNER

SWEET TREATS ON A BUDGET

MONDAY
Rhubarb Slumps (see page 26)

TUESDAY
Tipsy Berry Waffles (see page 38)

WEDNESDAY
Fig & Honey Pots (see page 54)

THURSDAY
Coconut Syllabub & Almond Brittle (see page 110)

FRIDAY
Blackberry & Apple Puffs (see page 40)

SATURDAY
Sticky Sultana & Bran Slice (see page 36)

STORECUPBOARD

The only extras you will need!

1 Sugars
2 Flours
3 Oils & vinegars
4 Baking powder
5 Bicarbonate of soda
6 Salt
7 Lemons & lemon juice

SUNDAY
Chocolate Apple Pancakes (see page 84)

(see page 84)

SHOPPING LIST:

Fruit, nuts & spices
- 400 g (13 oz) rhubarb
- 250 g (8 oz) mixed berries, such as blueberries, blackberries and raspberries
- 8 ripe fresh figs
- 2 tablespoons chopped pistachio nuts
- 50 g (2 oz) flaked almonds
- 125 g (4 oz) blackberries
- 4 dessert apples
- 200 g (7 oz) sultanas
- 15 cardamom seeds, lightly crushed
- 3 tsp ground cinnamon
- 1 teaspoon ground mixed spice

Dairy
- 215 g (7½ oz) unsalted butter, softened
- 15 g (½ oz) butter
- 400 ml (14 fl oz) double cream
- 4 tablespoons crème fraîche
- 450 ml (¾ pint) Greek yogurt
- 500 ml (17 fl oz) milk
- 7 eggs

Bottles, tins & packets
- 100 g (3½ oz) oats
- 100 g (3½ oz) granulated sugar
- 125 g (4 oz) demerara sugar
- 125 g (4 oz) caster sugar
- icing sugar
- 6 tablespoons golden caster sugar
- 2 tablespoons dark muscovado sugar
- 75 g (3 oz) plain flour
- 150 g (5 oz) self-raising flour
- 2 tablespoons vegetable oil
- 200 ml (7 fl oz) coconut cream
- 4 tablespoons clear honey
- 2 tablespoons black treacle
- 100 g (3½ oz) bran flake cereal
- 2 tablespoons kirsch
- ready-made waffles and pancakes
- 4 tablespoons chocolate and hazelnut spread

5 FOR COOLING OFF

What's your favourite way to cool off? Whether you're looking for something refreshing or want to impress guests with a chilled treat, these 5-ingredient recipes prove that frozen desserts can be simple to make.

Tropical Fruit & Basil Ice Cream (see page 28)

Rocky Road Ice Cream Sundaes (see page 122)

Frozen Berry Yoghurt Ice Cream (see page 152)

Instant Raspberry Sorbet (see page 58)

Chocolate Ice Cream (see page 68)

5 FOR WARMING UP

For chilly autumn evenings and cold winter nights, this selection of cakes and desserts will provide comfort for any afternoon or evening, and all using only 5 key ingredients!

Steamed Apple Pudding (see page 126)

Rich Chocolate Brownies (see page 150)

Sticky Toffee & Date Squares (see page 184)

Sweet Cranberry & Orange Pie (see page 56)

Lemon Puddle Pudding (see page 34)

5 FOR MAKING WITH THE KIDS

Cooking and baking is a great opportunity to teach kids all sorts of valuable skills and these recipes with only 5 or less main ingredients are perfect starting points. Have some fun with the kids in the kitchen and get them involved with these easy recipes.

Mile-high Marshmallow Cupcakes (see page 80)

Peanut Butter Cookies (see page 140)

Iced Fig Slice (see page 114)

Baby Butterflies (see page 172)

Chocolate Puddle Pudding (see page 82)

5 FOR AFTERNOON TEA

Any of these recipes would make the perfect centrepiece to a traditional English afternoon tea served with pots of tea and cucumber sandwiches, and with only 5 or less ingredients they couldn't be simpler.

Chocolate Caramel Shortbread (see page 74)

Chai Teabread (see page 104)

Strawberry Lavender Shortbread (see page 116)

Vienesse Whirls (see page 174)

French Macaroons (see page 180)

5 FOR A SUMMER PICNIC

These lunchbox or picnic-friendly recipes are perfect for taking al fresco and enjoying in the great outdoors. Just try not to eat them en route!

Fruited Friands (see page 44)

White Chocolate & Apricot Blondies (see page 78)

Fairings (see page 136)

Mini Custard Tarts (see page 168)

Marsala Raisin Coffee Muffins (see page 178)

5 DINNER PARTY TREATS

Impress your guests with these showstopping desserts, and all using only 5 or less key ingredients!

Chilled Blackcurrant & Mint Soufflés
(see page 42)

Classic Lemon Tart (see page 102)

Sweet Chestnut Mess (see page 106)

Coconut Syllabub (see page 110)

Mini Baked Alaskas (see page 138)

FRUITY

Preparation time 20 minutes, plus chilling
Cooking time 25–30 minutes

INGREDIENTS

1	375 g (12 oz) ready-made puff pastry
2	2 crisp green dessert apples (such as Granny Smith), peeled, cored and sliced
3	25 g (1 oz) unsalted butter, chilled
4	ice cream, to serve
5	250 g (8 oz) apricot jam, to glaze

STORECUPBOARD

1 tablespoon caster sugar; 2 teaspoons lemon juice;
2 teaspoons water

French Apple Flan

■ Divide the pastry into quarters and roll each out on a lightly floured surface until 2 mm (⅛ inch) thick. Using a 13 cm (5½ inch) plate as a guide, cut out 4 rounds – make a number of short cuts around the plate rather than drawing the knife around, which can stretch the pastry. Place the rounds on a baking sheet.

■ Place a slightly smaller plate on each pastry round and score around the edge to form a 1 cm (½ inch) border. Prick the centres with a fork and chill for 30 minutes.

■ Arrange the apple slices in a circle over the pastry rounds and sprinkle with the sugar. Grate the butter over the top and bake in a preheated oven, 220°C (425°F), Gas Mark 7, for 25–30 minutes until the pastry and apples are golden.

■ Meanwhile, make an apricot glaze. Put the jam in a small saucepan with the lemon juice and water and heat gently until the jam melts. Increase the heat and boil for 1 minute, remove from the heat and press through a fine sieve. Keep warm, then brush over each apple tart while they are still warm. Serve with ice cream.

A PEACHY DELIGHT

For peach tartlets, replace the 2 apples with 2 peaches, halved, skinned and thinly sliced. Arrange on the pastry rounds and continue as opposite, baking for 12–15 minutes.

SERVES 8

Preparation time 20 minutes, plus chilling
Cooking time 33–40 minutes

INGREDIENTS

1 400 g (13 oz) chilled ready-made or homemade sweet shortcrust pastry

2 200 ml (7 fl oz) freshly squeezed lime juice (4–6 limes)

3 8 kaffir lime leaves or the grated rind of 3 limes

4 3 eggs plus 2 egg yolks

5 175 g (6 oz) unsalted butter, softened

STORECUPBOARD

a little flour, for dusting; 175 g (6 oz) caster sugar; icing sugar, for dusting

Kaffir Lime Tart

■ Roll out the pastry on a lightly floured surface and use it to line a 23 cm (9 inch) flan tin. Prick the base with a fork and chill for 30 minutes.

■ Line with nonstick baking paper, add baking beans and bake blind in a preheated oven, 200°C (400°F), Gas Mark 6, for 15 minutes. Remove the paper and beans and bake for a further 12–15 minutes until the pastry is crisp and golden. Set aside to cool.

■ Make the filling. Put the sugar, lime juice and kaffir lime leaves or lime rind in a saucepan and heat gently to dissolve the sugar. Bring to the boil and simmer for 5 minutes. Leave to cool for 5 minutes, then strain into a clean pan.

■ Stir in the eggs, egg yolks and half the butter and heat gently, stirring, for 1 minute or until the sauce coats the back of the spoon. Add the remaining butter and whisk constantly until the mixture thickens.

■ Transfer the lime mixture to the pastry case and bake for 6–8 minutes until set. Leave to cool and serve warm dusted with icing sugar.

ADD MORE FRUIT

For mango & kiwifruit salad, to serve with the tart, peel, stone and dice 1 large mango, then mix with 3 peeled and sliced kiwifruits, the seeds scooped from 3 passion fruits and the juice of 1 lime.

SERVES 4

Preparation time 10 minutes
Cooking time 20–25 minutes

INGREDIENTS

1 400 g (13 oz) rhubarb, cut into chunks

2 grated rind and juice of 1 orange

3 175 g (6 oz) unsalted butter, softened

4 100 g (3½ oz) oats

5 6 tablespoons double cream

STORECUPBOARD

6 tablespoons golden caster sugar; 2 tablespoons
dark muscovado sugar

Rhubarb Slumps

■ Mix together the rhubarb, golden caster
sugar and orange rind and half the juice in
a bowl. Spoon the mixture into 4 individual
ramekins.

■ Put the oats, cream, dark muscovado
sugar and remaining orange juice in the
bowl and mix together. Drop spoonfuls of
the oat mixture all over the surface of the
rhubarb mixture.

■ Set the ramekins on a baking sheet and
bake in a preheated oven, 180°C (350°F),
Gas Mark 4, for 20–25 minutes until the
topping is browned. Serve hot.

MAKE IT CRUMBLY

For apple and blackberry crumbles, peel, core and chop 2 dessert apples, then mix with 100 g (3½ oz) blackberries, 6 tablespoons golden caster sugar and 1 tablespoon apple juice. Spoon into the ramekins as above. Sift 125 g (4 oz) plain flour into a bowl, add 50 g (2 oz) diced butter and rub in with the fingertips until the mixture resembles coarse breadcrumbs. Stir in 50 g (2 oz) dark muscovado sugar, 25 g (1 oz) bran flakes and 50 g (2 oz) chopped mixed nuts. Spoon the mixture over the fruit and flatten slightly with the back of a spoon. Bake as opposite until the topping is lightly golden.

SERVES 4–6

Preparation time 10 minutes
Cooking time none

INGREDIENTS

1 450 g (14 oz) frozen tropical fruits, such as mango, papaya and pineapple

2 1 tablespoon lime juice

3 200 g (7 oz) mascarpone cheese

4 2 tablespoons chopped basil, plus 4–6 basil sprigs, to decorate

STORECUPBOARD

2 tablespoons icing sugar

Tropical Fruit & Basil Ice Cream

■ Place half the fruit and the lime juice in a food processor and whizz until roughly chopped. Add the mascarpone and icing sugar and blend until fairly smooth.

■ Add the remaining fruit and the basil and pulse until no large lumps of fruit remain. Scoop into bowls and serve immediately, decorated with basil sprigs.

INGREDIENTS

1 40 g (1½ oz) unsalted butter

2 1 egg, plus 1 egg yolk

3 few drops vanilla essence

4 150 ml (¼ pint) mixed milk and water

5 410 g (13½ oz) can apricot halves, drained

STORECUPBOARD

50 g (2 oz) plain flour; 2 tablespoons caster sugar;
grated rind of ½ lemon; icing sugar, for dusting

Apricot Clafouti

■ Sift the flour into a bowl and add the
sugar and lemon rind. Melt 25 g (1 oz) of
the butter, then add to the flour with the
whole egg, egg yolk and vanilla essence.
Gradually whisk in the milk and water
until smooth. Leave to stand for 30 minutes
or longer.

■ Grease liberally 4 individual 200 ml
(7 fl oz) metal pudding moulds with the
remaining butter. Quarter the apricots and
divide among the tins. Stand the tins on a
baking sheet, then cook in a preheated oven,
190°C (375°F), Gas Mark 5, for 5 minutes.

■ Pour the batter quickly into the pudding
moulds so that the mix sizzles in the hot
butter. Bake for about 20 minutes until well
risen and golden brown. Dust the tops with
sifted icing sugar and serve immediately,
as the puddings sink as they cool.

TRY CHERRIES

For cherry clafouti, make the batter with the grated rind of ½ orange instead of the lemon. Drain a 350 g (11 oz) jar of morello cherries in syrup and divide the cherries between the pudding moulds as opposite. Bake the fruit and then add the batter as opposite.

Preparation time 25 minutes, plus cooling
Cooking time 1 hour 5 minutes

INGREDIENTS

1 2 × 425 g (14 oz) cans pitted black or red cherries

2 1 teaspoon ground mixed spice

3 175 g (6 oz) slightly salted butter, chilled and diced

4 50 g (2 oz) ground almonds

5 1 egg

STORECUPBOARD

2 teaspoons cornflour; 250 g (8 oz) self-raising flour; 175 g (6 oz) golden caster sugar

Cherry Crumble Cake

■ Drain the cherries, reserving 7 tablespoons of the juice. Put a little of the reserved juice in a small saucepan with the cornflour and blend until smooth. Add the remaining juice and bring to the boil, stirring. Add the cherries and cook, stirring, for about 1 minute or until thickened slightly. Leave to cool.

■ Put the flour and mixed spice in a bowl or food processor. Add the butter and rub in with fingertips or process until the mixture resembles breadcrumbs. Add the sugar and ground almonds and mix or blend again until the mixture resembles a coarse crumble. Reserve 200 g (7 oz) of the mixture. Add the egg to the remaining mixture and mix to a soft dough.

■ Turn the dough into a greased 22–23 cm (8½–9 inch) square shallow baking tin and press it into the corners and slightly up the sides. Spread over the cherries to 1.5 cm (¾ inch) from the edges, then sprinkle with the reserved crumble mixture.

■ Bake in a preheated oven, 180°C (350°F), Gas Mark 4, for about 1 hour until the crumble is golden. Leave to cool in the tin, then cut into squares.

USE APRICOTS

For apricot crumble cake, put 225 g (7½ oz) roughly chopped ready-to-eat dried apricots, 150 ml (¼ pint) apple or orange juice and 1½ teaspoons ground ginger in a saucepan. Bring to the boil, then reduce the heat and cook very gently for 5 minutes. Blend 1½ teaspoons cornflour with 2 tablespoons water and add to the pan. Cook, stirring, for 2 minutes until thickened slightly. Leave to cool. Make the cake opposite, omitting the mixed spice and using the apricot mixture instead of the cherries.

Preparation time 20 minutes
Cooking time 25 minutes

INGREDIENTS

 75 g (3 oz) unsalted butter, at room temperature

 3 eggs, separated

3 **300 ml (½ pint) milk**

STORECUPBOARD

150 g (5 oz) caster sugar; grated rind of 2 lemons, plus juice from 1 lemon; 50 g (2 oz) self-raising flour; icing sugar, for dusting (optional)

Lemon Puddle Pudding

■ Use some of the butter to lightly grease a 1.2 litre (2 pint) pie dish, then stand the dish in a roasting tin. Put the rest of the butter in a mixing bowl with the caster sugar and lemon rind. Whisk the egg whites in a separate bowl until they are softly peaking. Using the still dirty whisk, beat the butter, sugar and lemon rind until light and fluffy, then mix in the flour and egg yolks.

■ Mix in the milk and lemon juice gradually until only just mixed. The mixture may appear to separate slightly but this will disappear during baking.

■ Fold in the egg whites, then gently pour the mix into the greased dish. Pour hot water from the tap into the roasting tin to come halfway up the sides of the dish.

■ Cook in a preheated oven, 190°C (375°F), Gas Mark 5, for about 25 minutes until slightly risen, golden brown and the

top has begun to crack. Insert a knife into the centre – the top two-thirds should be soufflé-like and the bottom third a saucy, custard-like layer. If it's very soft in the centre, cook for an extra 5 minutes.

■ Dust the top with a little sifted icing sugar, if liked, then serve immediately spooned into shallow bowls. Don't leave the dessert to stand or the topping will absorb the sauce.

MAKE IT ORANGE

For Grand Marnier pudding, use the grated rind of 1 large orange instead of the lemon rind and replace the lemon juice with 3 tablespoons Grand Marnier. Cook as opposite.

Preparation time 10 minutes, plus standing
Cooking time 45 minutes

INGREDIENTS

1	200 g (7 oz) sultanas
2	2 tablespoons black treacle
3	100 g (3½ oz) shredded bran or bran flake cereal
4	1 teaspoon ground mixed spice
5	300 ml (½ pint) milk

STORECUPBOARD

125 g (4 oz) demerara sugar, plus extra for sprinkling; 150 g (5 oz) self-raising flour

Sticky Sultana & Bran Slice

■ Mix together the sultanas, sugar, treacle, bran, mixed spice and milk in a bowl. Leave to stand for 20 minutes to allow the bran to soften. Stir in the flour.

■ Tip the mixture into a greased and lined 1 kg (2 lb) or 1.3 litre (2¼ pint) loaf tin and level the surface. Bake in a preheated oven, 160°C (325°F), Gas Mark 3, for about 45 minutes or until risen, firm to the touch and a skewer inserted into the centre comes out clean. Loosen the cake at the ends and transfer to a wire rack. Peel off the lining paper and leave to cool. Cut into slices and spread with a little butter to serve.

ADD FIGS

For gingered fig slice, make the cake as opposite, replacing the sultanas with 200 g (7 oz) sliced dried figs, the black treacle with 2 tablespoons clear honey and the mixed spice with 1 piece of slem ginger in syrup, finely chopped. Serve drizzled with extra honey.

SERVES 4

Preparation time 5 minutes
Cooking time 1–2 minutes

INGREDIENTS

1	15 g (½ oz) butter
2	250 g (8 oz) mixed berries, such as blueberries, blackberries and raspberries
3	2 tablespoons kirsch
4	4 waffles
5	4 tablespoons crème fraîche

STORECUPBOARD

1 tablespoon caster sugar

Tipsy Berry Waffles

■ Melt the butter in a nonstick frying pan, add the berries, sugar and kirsch and cook over a high heat, stirring gently, for 1–2 minutes.

■ Meanwhile, toast or reheat the waffles according to the packet instructions. Put a waffle on each serving plate, spoon the berries over the waffles and top each portion with 1 tablespoon crème fraîche. Serve immediately.

SERVES 6

Preparation time 15 minutes
Cooking time 20 minutes

INGREDIENTS

1	1 tsp ground cinnamon
2	200 ml (7 fl oz) milk
3	2 large eggs
4	125 g (4 oz) blackberries
5	1 small dessert apple, cored and cut into thin slices

STORECUPBOARD

2 tablespoons vegetable oil; 75 g (3 oz) plain flour; pinch of salt; 50 g (2 oz) caster sugar, plus 1 tablespoon; icing sugar, for dusting

Blackberry & Apple Puffs

■ Liberally brush a 12-hole bun tin with the oil. Place in a preheated oven, 180°C (350°F), Gas Mark 4 to heat.

■ Meanwhile, sift the flour, cinnamon and salt into a large bowl. Stir in the 50 g (2 oz) sugar and make a well in the centre. Whisk together the milk and eggs in a jug, then gradually whisk into the flour to form a smooth batter.

■ Remove the hot bun tin from the oven and pour in the batter. Add a couple of blackberries in the centres, then top with apple slices and sprinkle with the 1 tablespoon sugar.

■ Return to the oven and cook for 20 minutes or until risen, golden and cooked through. Serve dusted with icing sugar.

ADD A SAUCE

For a blackberry sauce, place 300 g (10 oz) blackberries, 2 tablespoons caster sugar and the grated rind and juice of 1 lemon in a saucepan and heat gently for 5–6 minutes until the fruit starts to burst. Serve warm with spoonfuls of vanilla yogurt.

SERVES 6

Preparation time 40 minutes, plus chilling
Cooking time 18–20 minutes

INGREDIENTS

1 250 g (8 oz) blackcurrants, defrosted if frozen

2 4 teaspoons powdered gelatine

3 4 eggs, separated

4 250 ml (8 fl oz) double cream

5 5 tablespoons finely chopped fresh mint

STORECUPBOARD

6 tablespoons water; 200 g (7 oz) caster sugar; icing sugar, for dusting

Chilled Blackcurrant & Mint Soufflé

■ Wrap a double thickness strip of nonstick baking paper around a 13 cm (5½ inch) diameter × 6 cm (2½ inch) deep soufflé dish so the paper stands 6 cm (2½ inches) above the dish top. Put the blackcurrants and 2 tablespoons of the water in a saucepan, cover and cook gently for 5 minutes until softened. Blend until smooth, then press through a sieve.

■ Put the remaining water in a small heatproof bowl and sprinkle over the gelatine, making sure the water absorbs all the powder. Set aside for 5 minutes, then stand the bowl in a pan half-filled with boiling water and simmer for 3–4 minutes, stirring occasionally, until the gelatine dissolves to a clear liquid.

■ Put the egg yolks and caster sugar in a large heatproof bowl and place over a pan of simmering water making sure the base of the bowl is not touching the water.

Whisk for 10 minutes or until the egg yolks are very thick and pale, and leave a trail when lifted above the mixture. Remove from the heat and continue whisking until cool. Fold in the dissolved gelatine in a thin, steady stream, then fold in the purée.

■ Whip the cream softly, then fold into the soufflé mix with the mint. Whisk the whites into stiff, moist-looking peaks. Fold a large spoonful into the soufflé mixture to loosen it, then gently fold in the remaining whites. Pour the mixture into the soufflé dish so that it stands above the rim of the dish. Chill for 4 hours or until set.

■ Remove the string and paper. To decorate, arrange 4–5 strips of nonstick baking paper over the soufflé top so some overlap, then dust with sifted icing sugar. Lift off the strips and serve immediately or the sugar will dissolve.

Preparation time 20 minutes, plus cooling
Cooking time 25 minutes

INGREDIENTS

1 175 g (6 oz) unsalted butter

2 75 g (3 oz) dried strawberries, sour cherries or cranberries roughly chopped

3 2 tablespoons orange juice

4 6 egg whites

5 125 g (4 oz) ground almonds

STORECUPBOARD

225 g (7½ oz) caster sugar, plus extra for sprinkling; 75 g (3 oz) plain flour

Fruited Friands

■ Melt the butter and leave to cool. Put the dried strawberries, cherries or cranberries and orange juice in a saucepan and heat until hot, then tip into a bowl and leave to cool.

■ Whisk the egg whites in a large clean bowl with a hand-held electric whisk until frothy and increased in volume but not peaking. Add the sugar, flour and ground almonds and stir in until almost combined. Drizzle the melted butter over the mixture, then stir together gently until just combined.

■ Divide the mixture evenly between the holes of a greased 12-hole muffin tray, then scatter the strawberries, cherries or cranberries on top. Bake in a preheated oven, 200°C (400°F), Gas Mark 6, for about 20 minutes until pale golden and

just firm to the touch. Leave in the tin for 5 minutes, then transfer to a wire rack to cool. Serve sprinkled with caster sugar.

A NUTTY VERSION

For hazelnut friands, put 125 g (4 oz) blanched hazelnuts in a food processor or blender and whizz until the consistency of ground almonds. Finely chop a further 25 g (1 oz) hazelnuts. Make the friands as opposite, adding ½ teaspoon ground cinnamon when melting the butter, omitting the strawberries and orange juice and replacing the ground almonds with the ground hazelnuts. Spoon the mixture into the tray and scatter with the chopped hazelnuts. Bake as opposite.

SERVES 8

Preparation time 40 minutes, plus freezing
Cooking time 20–25 minutes

INGREDIENTS

1	**75 g (3 oz) unsalted butter**
2	**½ teaspoon ground mixed spice**
3	**3 small mangoes, peeled, pitted and thickly sliced**
4	**350 g (12 oz) chilled ready-made puff pastry**

STORECUPBOARD

75 g (3 oz) palm sugar, grated, or light soft brown sugar; a little flour, for dusting

Mango & Palm Sugar Tatin

■ Make the topping. Heat the butter, sugar and spice together in a 23 cm (9 inch) ovenproof frying pan until the butter has melted. Remove the pan from the heat. Carefully arrange the mango slices in the pan, fanning them from the centre outwards, to make 2 layers.

■ Roll out the pastry on a lightly floured surface and trim to a round a little larger than the size of the pan. Press it down over the mangoes and into the edges of the pan and pierce a small hole in the centre. Bake in a preheated oven, 220°C (425°F), Gas Mark 7, for 20–25 minutes until the pastry is risen and golden. Leave to stand for 10 minutes before turning out on to a large plate.

MAKES 4

Preparation time 30 minutes
Cooking time 20–25 minutes

INGREDIENTS

1 400 g (13 oz) gooseberries, topped and tailed

2 375 g (12 oz) sweet shortcrust pastry

3 1 tablespoon elderflower cordial, undiluted

4 milk or beaten egg, to glaze

STORECUPBOARD

125 g (4 oz) caster sugar, plus extra for sprinkling;
2 teaspoons cornflour

Gooseberry & Elderflower Pies

■ Mix the sugar, cornflour and gooseberries together in a bowl. Cut the pastry into 4 pieces, then roll each piece out to about an 18 cm (7 inch) circle. Drape each piece into a buttered individual Yorkshire pudding tin, 10 cm (4 inches) in diameter and 2.5 cm (1 inch) deep, leaving the excess pastry overhanging the edges of the tins.

■ Spoon in the gooseberry mixture and mound up in the centre, then drizzle over the elderflower cordial. Fold the overhanging pastry up and over the filling, pleating where needed and leaving the centres of the pies open.

■ Brush the pastry with milk or beaten egg, sprinkle with a little sugar and bake in a preheated oven, 190°C (375°F), Gas Mark 5, for 20–25 minutes until golden. Leave to stand for 15 minutes, then serve with elderflower cream (see opposite).

MAKE AN ELDERFLOWER CREAM

For elderflower cream, to serve as an accompaniment, whip 200 ml (7 fl oz) double cream, then fold in 2 tablespoons undiluted elderflower cordial and the grated rind of ½ lemon.

Preparation time 30 minutes
Cooking time 20–25 minutes

INGREDIENTS

| 1 | 500 g (1 lb) chilled ready-made puff pastry |

| 2 | 4 ripe peaches or nectarines, thickly sliced |

| 3 | 125 g (4 oz) blueberries |

| 4 | 1 egg, beaten |

STORECUPBOARD

a little flour, for dusting; 50 g (2 oz) caster sugar, plus extra to decorate; grated rind of ½ lemon; icing sugar, for dusting

Peach & Blueberry Jalousie

■ Roll out half the pastry on a lightly floured surface and trim to a 30 × 18 cm (12 × 7 inch) rectangle. Transfer to a lightly greased baking sheet.

■ Pile the peach or nectarine slices on top, leaving a 2.5 cm (1 inch) border of pastry showing, then sprinkle on the blueberries, sugar and lemon rind. Brush the pastry border with a little beaten egg.

■ Roll out the remaining pastry to a little larger than the first piece, then trim to 33 × 20 cm (13 × 8 inches). Fold in half lengthways, then make cuts in from the fold about 1 cm (½ inch) apart and about 6 cm (2½ inches) long, leaving a wide uncut border of pastry.

■ Lift the pastry over the fruit, unfold so that the fruit and bottom layer of pastry are completely covered, then press the pastry edges together. Trim if needed.

■ Knock up the pastry edges with a knife, then flute the edges by pressing the first and second finger on to the pie edge, then make small cuts with a knife between them to create a scalloped edge.

■ Brush the top of the pastry with beaten egg, sprinkle with a little extra sugar and bake in a preheated oven, 200°C (400°F), Gas Mark 6, for 20–25 minutes until the pastry is well risen and golden brown. Serve cut into squares, warm or cold.

A SEASONAL FILLING

For apple & blackberry jalousie,
replace the peaches and blueberries
with 4 Granny Smith apples, cored,
quartered and thickly sliced, and
125 g (4 oz) blackberries.

CUTS INTO 8

Preparation time 40 minutes
Cooking time 35–45 minutes

INGREDIENTS

1   4 egg whites

2   ¼ teaspoon cream of tartar

3   50 g (2 oz) walnut pieces, lightly toasted and chopped

4   200 ml (7 fl oz) double cream

5   250 g (8 oz) strawberries

STORECUPBOARD

125 g (4 oz) light muscovado sugar; 100 g (3½ oz) caster sugar; 1 teaspoon white wine vinegar

Strawberry Macaroon Cake

■ Whisk the egg whites and cream of tartar in a large clean bowl until stiff. Combine the sugars then gradually whisk into the egg white, a little at a time, until it has all been added. Whisk for a few minutes more until the meringue mixture is thick and glossy. Fold in the white wine vinegar, then fold in the walnuts.

■ Divide the meringue mixture evenly between 2 greased 20 cm (8 inch) sandwich tins, base-lined with nonstick baking paper. Spread the surfaces level then swirl the tops with the back of a spoon. Bake in a preheated oven, 150°C (300°F), Gas Mark 2, for 35–45 minutes until lightly browned and crisp. Loosen the edges and leave to cool in the tins.

■ Re-loosen the edges of the meringues and turn out on to 2 clean tea towels. Peel off the lining paper then put one of the meringues on a serving plate.

■ Whip the cream until softly peaking, then spoon three-quarters over the meringue. Halve 8 of the smallest strawberries and set aside. Hull and slice the rest and arrange on the cream. Cover with the second meringue, top uppermost. Decorate with spoonfuls of the remaining cream and the reserved halved strawberries. Serve within 2 hours of assembly.

SERVES 4

Preparation time 10 minutes, plus chilling
Cooking time none

INGREDIENTS

1   6 ripe fresh figs, thinly sliced

2   450 ml (¾ pint) Greek yogurt

3   4 tablespoons clear honey

4   2 tablespoons chopped pistachio nuts

Fig & Honey Pots

■ Arrange the fig slices snugly in the bottom of 4 glasses or glass bowls. Spoon the yogurt over the figs and chill in the refrigerator for 10–15 minutes.

■ Just before serving, drizzle 1 tablespoon honey over each dessert and sprinkle the pistachio nuts on top.

Preparation time 30 minutes, plus cooling
Cooking time 35-40 minutes

INGREDIENTS

1 500 g (1 lb) frozen cranberries

2 grated rind and juice of 1½ oranges

3 500 g (1 lb) ready-made puff pastry, defrosted if frozen

4 beaten egg, to glaze

STORECUPBOARD

150 g (5 oz) caster sugar; 2 tablespoons water; 1 tablespoon cornflour; 100 g (3½ oz) sifted icing sugar

Sweet Cranberry & Orange Pie

■ Cook the cranberries in a saucepan with the sugar, rind and juice from 1 orange (reserving the rest for decoration) and the measurement water for 10 minutes, stirring occasionally until the cranberries are soft. Mix the cornflour to a paste with a little extra water, add to the cranberries and cook for a few minutes, stirring until thickened, then leave to cool.

■ Cut the pastry in half, roll out one half on a lightly floured surface and trim to a 20 × 25 cm (8 × 10 inch) rectangle, then transfer to a buttered baking sheet. Brush the egg in a border around the edge of the rectangle, then pile the cranberry mixture in the middle.

■ Roll out the remaining pastry a little larger than the first and drape over the cranberries. Press the pastry edges together to seal well, then trim the top

pastry layer to match the lower one. Knock up the edges of the pastry, then flute.

■ Brush the top with egg, then bake in a preheated oven, 200°F (400°F), Gas Mark 6, for 25-30 minutes until well risen and golden brown. Leave to cool for 30 minutes.

■ Mix the icing sugar with enough of the remaining orange juice to make a smooth icing that just falls from a spoon, then drizzle randomly over the pie to decorate and sprinkle with the remaining grated orange rind. Set aside for 20 minutes or until the icing is set, then cut into strips to serve.

TRY MIXED BERRIES

For mixed berry pie, cook a
500 g (1 lb) bag of mixed frozen
blackberries, cherries and currants
with 100 g (3½ oz) caster sugar and
the rind and juice of 1 orange, but no
extra water. Thicken with cornflour
and finish as above, dusting the top
with icing sugar instead of the icing.

SERVES 4

Preparation time 5 minutes
Cooking time none

INGREDIENTS

1   300 g (10 oz) frozen raspberries

2   1 tablespoon crème de framboise
     (raspberry liqueur) (optional)

3   fresh raspberries, to serve

STORECUPBOARD

2 tablespoons caster sugar; 2 tablespoons water

Instant Raspberry Sorbet

■ Place the raspberries, sugar, measurement water and crème de framboise, if using, in a food processor. Blitz for 2–3 minutes until all the ingredients are blended and start to come together.

■ Serve scoops of sorbet immediately in bowls with fresh raspberries or place in a freezerproof container and freeze until ready to use.

SERVE WITH CHOCOLATE CONES

Melt 50 g (2 oz) plain dark chocolate, broken into small pieces, in a heatproof bowl set over a saucepan of gently simmering water. Remove from the heat and dip the ends of 4 waffle cones into the melted chocolate, then roll the ends in 50 g (2 oz) chopped pistachios. Stand in glasses and chill until set. Make the raspberry sorbet as opposite and serve scoops in the cones.

Preparation time 20 minutes
Cooking time 35 minutes

INGREDIENTS

1   125 g (4 oz) unsalted butter, softened

2   2 large eggs, beaten

3   100 g (3½ oz) ground almonds

4   3 ripe pears, peeled, halved and cored

5   50 g (2 oz) flaked almonds

STORECUPBOARD

125 g (4 oz) caster sugar; 50 g (2 oz) plain flour,
sifted; ½ teaspoon baking powder; sifted icing
sugar, for dusting

Pear & Almond Cake

■ Beat together the butter and caster
sugar in a bowl until pale and fluffy. Add
the eggs, a little at a time, beating well
after each addition. If the mixture starts to
curdle, add 1 tablespoon of the flour. Fold
in the flour, ground almonds and baking
powder using a large metal spoon.

■ Spoon the mixture into a greased 20 cm
(8 inch) spring-form cake tin and level the
surface. Arrange the pear halves over the
top and bake in a preheated oven,
190°C (375°F), Gas Mark 5, for 25 minutes.
Sprinkle the flaked almonds over the
top and return to the oven for a further
10 minutes until a skewer inserted into
the centre comes out clean.

■ Leave to cool in the tin, then carefully
remove the ring and base and dust with
icing sugar. Serve with Mascarpone, Marsala
& Orange Cream, if desired (see opposite).

ADD A SWEET CREAM

For mascarpone, Marsala & orange cream, to serve as an accompaniment, whisk together the grated rind of 1 orange and 2 tablespoons orange juice, 2 tablespoons sweet Marsala and 100 g (3½ oz) mascarpone cheese in a bowl. Sweeten with sifted icing sugar to taste.

CHOCOLATE

Preparation time 10 minutes, plus cooling and setting
Cooking time 50–55 minutes

INGREDIENTS

1   **425 g (14 oz) plain dark chocolate, broken into pieces**

2   **200 g (7 oz) butter**

3   **4 eggs, beaten**

4   **150 ml (¼ pint) single cream**

STORECUPBOARD

125 g (4 oz) caster sugar;
225 g (7½ oz) self-raising flour, sifted

Easy Chocolate Fudge Cake

■ Grease a 20 × 30 cm (8 × 12 inch) baking tin lightly and line the base and sides with nonstick baking paper. Put 250 g (8 oz) of the chocolate with the butter in a heatproof bowl set over a saucepan of gently simmering water (don't let the bowl touch the water) and stir over a low heat until melted. Leave to cool for 5 minutes.

■ Whisk together the eggs and sugar in a bowl for 5 minutes until thick, while the cake is cooking. Beat in the cooled chocolate mixture and fold in the flour.

■ Spoon the mixture into the prepared tin and bake in a preheated oven, 160°C (325°F), Gas Mark 3, for 45–50 minutes until risen and firm to the touch. Leave to cool in the tin for 10 minutes, then turn out on to a wire rack to cool completely, removing the paper from the base.

■ Meanwhile, make the icing. Put the remaining 175 g (6 oz) chocolate in a saucepan with the cream and heat gently, stirring, until melted. Leave to cool for 1 hour until thickened to a pouring consistency, then spread over the cake. Leave to set for 30 minutes before serving.

MAKES 16

Preparation time 10 minutes
Cooking time 15 minutes

INGREDIENTS

1   125 g (4 oz) unsalted butter, softened

2   1 teaspoon vanilla extract

3   1 egg, lightly beaten

4   1 tablespoon milk

5   250 g (8 oz) plain dark chocolate chips

STORECUPBOARD

175 g (6 oz) soft light brown sugar; 200 g (7 oz) plain flour; 1 teaspoon baking powder

Chocolate Chip Cookies

■ Beat together the butter and sugar in a large bowl until pale and fluffy. Mix in the vanilla, then gradually beat in the egg, beating well after each addition. Stir in the milk. Sift in the flour and baking powder, then fold in. Stir in the chocolate chips.

■ Drop level tablespoonfuls of the mixture, about 3.5 cm (1½ inches) apart, on to a large baking sheet lined with baking parchment, then lightly press with a floured fork. Bake in a preheated oven, 180°C (350°F), Gas Mark 4, for 15 minutes or until lightly golden. Transfer to a wire rack to cool.

SERVES 4

Preparation time 20 minutes,
plus cooling and freezing
Cooking time 10 minutes

INGREDIENTS

1 300 ml (½ pint) double cream

2 2 tablespoons milk

3 ½ teaspoon vanilla essence

4 275 g (9 oz) good-quality plain dark chocolate, broken into pieces

5 2 tablespoons single cream

STORECUPBOARD

50 g (2 oz) icing sugar, sifted; 150 ml (¼ pint) water; 3 tablespoons caster sugar

Chocolate Ice Cream

■ Put the double cream and milk in a bowl and whisk until just stiff. Stir in the icing sugar and vanilla essence. Pour the mixture into a shallow freezer container and freeze for 30 minutes or until the ice cream begins to set around the edges. (This ice cream cannot be made in an ice-cream machine.)

■ Melt 125 g (4 oz) of the chocolate with the single cream in a heatproof bowl set over a pan of barely simmering water, making sure the base of the bowl does not touch the water. Stir until smooth, then set aside to cool.

■ Remove the ice cream from the freezer and spoon into a bowl. Add the melted chocolate and quickly stir it through the ice cream with a fork. Return the ice cream to the freezer container, cover and freeze until set. Transfer the ice cream to the refrigerator 30 minutes before serving, to soften slightly.

■ Heat the water, caster sugar and remaining chocolate together gently in a saucepan, stirring until melted. Serve immediately with scoops of the ice cream.

INGREDIENTS

1   8 g (¼ oz) mint leaves

2   125 g (4 oz) lightly salted butter, softened

3   2 eggs

4   175 g (6 oz) white chocolate, chopped

STORECUPBOARD

100 g (3½ oz) caster sugar; 150 g (5 oz) self-raising
flour; ½ teaspoon baking powder; icing sugar,
for dusting

Minted White Chocolate Cakes

■ Line a 12-section bun tin with paper
cake cases.

■ Put the mint leaves in a heatproof bowl,
cover with boiling water and leave for 30
seconds. Drain and pat dry on kitchen
paper. Put the leaves in a food processor
with the caster sugar and process until the
mint is finely chopped.

■ Transfer the mint sugar to a bowl and
add the butter, eggs, flour and baking
powder. Beat with a hand-held electric
whisk for about a minute until light and
creamy.

■ Stir in 100 g (3½ oz) of the chocolate
and then divide the cake mixture between
the paper cases. Scatter with the remaining
chocolate.

■ Bake in a preheated oven, 180°C
(350°F), Gas Mark 4, for 20 minutes or
until the cakes are risen and just firm to
the touch. Transfer to a wire rack to cool.
Lightly dust with icing sugar.

CUTS INTO 8

Preparation time 20 minutes
Cooking time 50 minutes

INGREDIENTS

1 125 g (4 oz) slightly salted butter, softened

2 2 eggs

3 25 g (1 oz) cocoa powder

4 150 g (5 oz) milk chocolate, chopped into 5 mm (¼ inch) pieces, plus an extra 50 g (2 oz), broken into pieces

5 50 g (2 oz) unsalted butter, softened

STORECUPBOARD

125 g (4 oz) light muscovado sugar; 125 g (4 oz) self-raising flour; 75 g (3 oz) golden icing sugar, sifted

Chocolate Chip Teabread

■ Grease a 500 g (1 lb) or 750 ml (1¼ pint) loaf tin and line with nonstick baking paper.

■ Beat together the salted butter, sugar, eggs, flour and cocoa powder in a bowl until smooth and creamy. Add 125 g (4 oz) of the chopped chocolate to the bowl. Mix well.

■ Spoon the mixture into the prepared tin and level the surface. Bake in a preheated oven, 160°C (325°F), Gas Mark 3, for about 50 minutes or until firm to the touch and a skewer inserted into the centre comes out clean. Loosen the cake at the ends and transfer to a wire rack. Peel off the lining paper and leave to cool.

■ Make the buttercream. Melt the broken pieces of chocolate in a heatproof bowl set over a saucepan of gently simmering water, making sure the base of the bowl does not touch the water. Meanwhile, beat together the unsalted butter and icing sugar in a bowl until pale and creamy. Beat in the melted chocolate. Spread the buttercream over the top of the cake and scatter with the reserved chopped chocolate.

CUTS INTO 15

Preparation time 20 minutes, plus chilling
Cooking time 15 minutes

INGREDIENTS

1	100 g (3½ oz) butter, at room temperature plus 100 g (3½ oz) butter
2	397 g (13 oz) can condensed milk
3	100 g (3½ oz) white chocolate, broken into pieces
4	100 g (3½ oz) plain dark chocolate, broken into pieces

STORECUPBOARD

50 g (2 oz) caster sugar; 100 g (3½ oz) brown rice flour; 100 g (3½ oz) cornflour; 50 g (2 oz) soft light brown sugar

Chocolate Caramel Shortbread

■ Beat 100 g (3½ oz) butter and caster sugar together in a mixing bowl until pale and creamy, then stir in the brown rice flour and cornflour until well combined. Press the shortbread into a 28 × 18 cm (11 × 7 inch) baking tin, then place in a preheated oven, 200°C (400°F), Gas Mark 6, for 10–12 minutes until golden.

■ Meanwhile, place the remaining butter, soft light brown sugar and condensed milk in a heavy-based saucepan and heat over a low heat until the sugar has dissolved, then cook for 5 minutes, stirring continuously until just beginning to darken. Remove from the heat and leave to cool a little, then pour the caramel over the shortbread base and leave to cool completely.

■ For the topping, melt the white and dark chocolate in separate heatproof bowls set over saucepans of simmering water,

making sure the base of the bowls do not touch the water. When the caramel is firm, spoon alternate spoonfuls of the white and dark chocolate over the caramel, tap the tin on the work surface so that the different chocolates merge, then use a knife to make swirls in the chocolate. Refrigerate until set, then cut into 15 pieces.

SERVES 4

Preparation time 10 minutes
Cooking time 13–18 minutes

INGREDIENTS

1   100 g (3½ oz) plain dark chocolate

2   3 eggs, separated

3   150 g (5 oz) raspberries, plus extra to
serve (optional)

STORECUPBOARD

50 g (2 oz) self-raising flour, sifted; 40 g (1½ oz)
caster sugar; icing sugar sifted, to decorate

Chocolate & Raspberry Soufflés

■ Break the chocolate into squares and
put them in a large heatproof bowl over
a saucepan of simmering water. Leave
until melted, then remove from the heat
and allow to cool a little. Whisk in the egg
yolks and fold in the flour.

■ Whisk the egg whites and caster sugar
in a medium bowl until they form soft
peaks. Beat a spoonful of the egg whites
into the chocolate mixture to loosen it
before gently folding in the rest.

■ Put the raspberries into 4 lightly greased
ramekins, pour over the chocolate mixture
and cook in a preheated oven, 190°C
(375°F), Gas Mark 5, for 12–15 minutes
until the soufflés have risen.

■ Sprinkle the soufflés with icing sugar
and serve with extra raspberries, if liked.

INGREDIENTS

1	300 g (10 oz) white chocolate
2	125 g (4 oz) butter
3	3 eggs
4	1 teaspoon vanilla essence
5	125 g (4 oz) ready-to-eat dried apricots, chopped

STORECUPBOARD

175 g (6 oz) caster sugar; 175 g (6 oz) self-raising flour; 1 teaspoon baking powder

White Chocolate & Apricot Blondies

■ Break half the chocolate into pieces, place in a saucepan with the butter and heat gently until melted. Dice the remaining chocolate.

■ Whisk the eggs, sugar and vanilla essence together in a bowl, using an electric whisk, for about 5 minutes until very thick and foamy and the whisk leaves a trail when lifted above the mixture. Fold in the melted chocolate mixture and then the flour and baking powder. Gently fold in half the chopped chocolate and apricots.

■ Pour the mixture into an 18 × 28 cm (7 × 11 inch) roasting tin lined with nonstick baking paper, and ease into the corners. Sprinkle with the remaining chocolate and apricots. Bake in a preheated oven, 180°C (350°F), Gas Mark 4, for 25–30 minutes until it is well risen, the top is crusty and the centre still slightly soft.

■ Leave to cool in the tin then lift out using the lining paper and cut into 20 small pieces. Peel off the paper and store in an airtight tin for up to 3 days.

CHANGE THE FRUIT

For white chocolate & cranberry blondies, follow the recipe opposite, simply replacing the ready-to-eat dried apricots with 75 g (3 oz) dried cranberries.

MAKES 12

Preparation time 25 minutes, plus cooling
Cooking time 25 minutes

INGREDIENTS

1 125 g (5 oz) marshmallows, plus extra chopped pieces to scatter

2 125 g (4 oz) lightly salted butter, softened

3 2 eggs

4 1 teaspoon vanilla extract

5 300 ml (½ pint) double cream

STORECUPBOARD

100 g (3½ oz) caster sugar; 150 g (5 oz) self-raising flour; ½ teaspoon baking powder

Mile-high Marshmallow Cupcakes

■ Line a 12-section bun tin with paper cake cases. Cut 50 g (2 oz) marshmallows into pieces using kitchen scissors.

■ Put the butter, sugar, eggs, flour, baking powder and vanilla in a bowl and beat with a hand-held electric whisk for about a minute until light and creamy. Stir in the chopped marshmallow pieces and then divide the cake mixture between the paper cases.

■ Bake in a preheated oven, 180°C (350°F), Gas Mark 4, for 20 minutes or until risen and just firm to the touch. Transfer to a wire rack to cool.

■ Cut the remaining marshmallows into small pieces and put about a third in a small saucepan with half the cream. Heat very gently until melted. Tip into a bowl and leave to cool.

■ Whip the remaining cream in a bowl until just holding its shape. Stir in the marshmallow cream and any remaining marshmallow pieces, then pile on to the cakes. Scatter with extra chopped marshmallow pieces to serve.

PRETTY IN PINK

For pink coconut cupcakes, grate 100 g (3½ oz) pink and white coconut ice. Make the cake mixture opposite, but add the grated coconut to the bowl with the other cake ingredients, use 50 g (2 oz) caster sugar rather than 100 g (3½ oz) and omit the marshmallows. Bake as opposite. Whip 200 ml (7 fl oz) double cream with 1 tablespoon icing sugar until just peaking. Pile on to the cooled cakes and scatter with extra grated coconut ice.

SERVES 4-6

Preparation time 15 minutes
Cooking time 15 minutes

INGREDIENTS

 1 75 g (3 oz) unsalted butter, at room
temperature

2 3 eggs

3 5 tablespoons cocoa powder

STORECUPBOARD

125 g (4 oz) light soft brown sugar;
65 g (2½ oz) self-raising flour; ½ teaspoon
baking powder; 250 ml (8 fl oz) boiling water;
icing sugar, to decorate

Chocolate Puddle Pudding

■ Rub a little of the butter all over the base and sides of a cooking dish and stand the dish on a baking sheet. Put the butter, 75 g (3 oz) light brown soft sugar and the eggs in a large bowl and sift in the flour, 3 tablespoons cocoa powder and the baking powder. Beat together until they form a smooth mixture. Spoon the pudding mixture into the dish and spread the top level.

■ To make a sauce, put the remaining 2 tablespoons cocoa powder and light brown soft sugar into a small bowl and mix in a little of the measurement boiling water to make a smooth paste. Gradually mix in the rest of the water, then pour the cocoa sauce over the pudding mixture.

■ Bake in a preheated oven, 180°C (350°F), Gas Mark 4, for 15 minutes or until the sauce has sunk to the bottom of the dish and the pudding is well risen. Sift a little icing sugar over the pudding before serving.

LITTLE PUDDINGS

For individual puddle puddings with orange cream, prepare the mixture as opposite and spoon it into 4 lightly greased ramekins. Bake as opposite for 10–12 minutes until the puddings are well risen. Mix clotted cream with a little finely grated orange rind and serve with the warm puddings.

SERVES 4

Preparation time 10 minutes
Cooking time 7–8 minutes

INGREDIENTS

1	40 g (1½ oz) unsalted butter
2	3 dessert apples, cored and thickly sliced
3	2 large pinches ground cinnamon
4	4 ready-made pancakes, about 20 cm (8 inches) in diameter
5	4 tablespoons chocolate and hazelnut spread

STORECUPBOARD

icing sugar, for dusting

Chocolate Apple Pancakes

■ Melt half the butter in a large frying pan, then add the apples and fry for 3–4 minutes, stirring and turning until hot and lightly browned. Sprinkle with the cinnamon.

■ Separate the pancakes, then spread with chocolate spread. Divide the apples among the pancakes, spooning them on to cover half of each pancake. Fold the uncovered sides over the apples.

■ Heat the remaining butter in the frying pan, add the pancakes and fry for a couple of minutes on each side to warm the pancakes through. Transfer to shallow plates and dust with sifted icing sugar.

CHANGE THE FRUIT

For peach melba pancakes, fry 2 large, thickly sliced peaches in the butter instead of the apples, omitting the cinnamon. Spread the pancakes with 4 tablespoons raspberry jam, then add the peaches and fold. Warm through, then serve sprinkled with fresh raspberries, a dusting of icing sugar and a scoop of ice cream.

Preparation time 20 minutes, plus chilling
Cooking time 15 minutes

INGREDIENTS

1	375 g (12 oz) chilled ready-made puff pastry
2	200 ml (7 fl oz) double cream
3	½ vanilla pod
4	200 g (7 oz) white chocolate, chopped
5	150 g (5 oz) raspberries

STORECUPBOARD

a little flour, for dusting; icing sugar, for dusting

White Chocolate & Raspberry Puffs

■ Roll out the pastry dough on a lightly floured surface until it is a rectangle 2.5 mm (⅛ inch) thick. Cut it into 6 rectangles, each 12 × 7 cm (5 × 3 inches), and put them on a baking sheet. Chill for 30 minutes. Bake in a preheated oven, 200°C (400°F), Gas Mark 6, for 15 minutes until the pastry is puffed and golden. Transfer to a wire rack to cool.

■ Put the cream and vanilla pod in a saucepan and heat gently until it reaches boiling point. Remove from the heat and scrape the seeds from the vanilla pod into the cream (discard the pod). Immediately stir in the chocolate and continue stirring until it has melted. Cool, chill for 1 hour until firm, then whisk until spreadable.

■ Split the pastries in half crossways and fill each with white chocolate cream and raspberries. Serve dusted with sifted icing sugar.

TRY STRAWBERRIES AND CREAM

For strawberry custard creams, make the pastry rectangles opposite then cool. Whip 150 ml (¼ pint) double cream until it forms soft swirls, then fold in a 125 g (4 oz) tub of ready-made custard. Split and fill the pastries with custard cream and 250 g (8 oz) sliced strawberries. Dust the tops with sifted icing sugar before serving.

DECADENT
TREATS

MAKES 12

Preparation time 30 minutes, plus cooling
Cooking time 25 minutes

INGREDIENTS

1   75 g (3 oz) flaked almonds

2   125 g (4 oz) lightly salted butter, softened

3   1 teaspoon vanilla extract

4   2 eggs

5   75 g (3 oz) unsalted butter, softened

STORECUPBOARD

sunflower oil, for brushing; 250 g (8 oz) caster sugar;
100 ml (3½ fl oz) water; 150 g (5 oz) self-raising flour;
½ teaspoon baking powder; 125 g (4 oz) icing sugar;
1 teaspoon hot water

Almond Praline Cupcakes

■ Line a 12-section bun tray with paper cake cases. Brush a baking sheet lightly with oil. Put 150 g (5 oz) of the caster sugar in a small, heavy-based saucepan with the water and heat gently until it has dissolved. Bring to the boil and boil rapidly until the syrup has turned to a pale golden caramel. Immediately stir in the flaked almonds. When coated, turn out on to the prepared baking sheet, spread in a thin layer and leave until cold and brittle.

■ Snap half the praline into jagged pieces and reserve. Process the remainder in a food processor until ground.

■ Put the salted butter, remaining caster sugar, vanilla extract, eggs, flour and baking powder in a bowl and beat with a hand-held electric whisk for about a minute until light and creamy. Stir in the ground praline. Divide the cake mixture between the paper cases.

■ Bake in a preheated oven, 180°C (350°F), Gas Mark 4, for 20 minutes or until risen and just firm to the touch. Transfer to a wire rack to cool.

■ Beat together the unsalted butter and icing sugar with the hot water in a bowl until pale and creamy. Spread over the cakes using a small palette knife. Decorate with the praline pieces.

Preparation time 10 minutes
Cooking time 10–15 minutes

INGREDIENTS

1   500 g (1 lb) nectarines, stoned and sliced

2   4 tablespoons orange liqueur, plus extra to flavour the fruit

3   350 ml (12 fl oz) soured cream

4   pinch of freshly grated nutmeg

5   1 teaspoon vanilla extract

STORECUPBOARD

125 g (4 oz) soft light brown sugar

Nectarine Brûlée

■ Put the nectarines in a saucepan and add enough water to cover. Poach over a low heat for 5–10 minutes, or until tender. Drain and divide between 6 individual ramekins. Stir in a little orange liqueur.

■ Beat together the soured cream, nutmeg, vanilla extract and the 4 tablespoons orange liqueur in a bowl until well combined. Spoon over the nectarine slices, then scatter the sugar over the top in a thick layer.

■ Cook under a preheated high grill until the sugar caramelizes.

Preparation time 25 minutes, plus cooling
Cooking time 55 minutes

INGREDIENTS

1 2 teaspoons egg white plus 2 eggs, separated

2 150 g (5 oz) shelled pistachio nuts

3 2 tablespoons vanilla sugar

4 125 g (4 oz) slightly salted butter, softened

STORECUPBOARD

100 g (3½ oz) caster sugar; finely grated rind of 1 lemon; 75 g (3 oz) plain flour; ½ teaspoon baking powder; sifted icing sugar, for dusting

Candied Pistachio Cake

■ Whisk the 2 teaspoons egg white in a bowl to break it up. Add the pistachio nuts and coat thinly in the egg white. Sprinkle in the vanilla sugar, turning the nuts to coat, then spread out on a baking sheet lined with baking parchment. Bake in a preheated oven, 160°C (325°F), Gas Mark 3, for 10 minutes. Leave to cool, then roughly chop.

■ Beat together the butter, 75 g (3 oz) of the caster sugar and the lemon rind in a bowl until very pale and fluffy. Beat in the egg yolks. Sift in the flour and baking powder, then stir in the nuts, reserving 3 tablespoons.

■ Whisk the egg whites in a clean bowl with a hand-held electric whisk until peaking. Gradually whisk in the remaining sugar, a spoonful at a time. Stir a third of the mixture into the creamed mixture

using a large metal spoon. Gently stir in the remaining egg whites.

■ Spoon the mixture into a greased and lined 1 kg (2 lb) or 1.3 litre (2¼ pint) loaf tin and level the surface. Scatter with the reserved nuts and bake in the oven for about 45 minutes or until firm to the touch and a skewer inserted into the centre comes out clean. Loosen the cake at the ends and transfer to a wire rack to cool. Peel off the lining paper and dust with sifted icing sugar.

SERVES 6

Preparation time 25 minutes,
plus soaking and chilling
Cooking time 5 minutes

INGREDIENTS

1 1 sachet or 3 teaspoons powdered
gelatine

2 500 ml (17 fl oz) rosé wine,
plus an extra 6 tablespoons

3 250 g (8 oz) small strawberries,
hulled and halved

4 250 ml (8 fl oz) double cream

STORECUPBOARD

4 tablespoons water; 65 g (2½ oz) caster sugar;
finely grated rind of 1 lemon

Strawberry Rosé Jelly & Syllabub

■ Spoon the measured water into a small
heatproof bowl or mug, then sprinkle
the gelatine over the top, tilting the bowl
so that the dry powder is completely
absorbed by the water. Leave to soak for
5 minutes.

■ Heat the bowl or mug in a small pan of
simmering water for 5 minutes or until a
clear liquid forms. Take off the heat, then
stir in 40 g (1½ oz) sugar until dissolved.
Cool slightly, then gradually mix into 500 ml
(17 fl oz) rosé wine.

■ Divide the strawberries between 6 tall
Champagne-style glasses. Pour the rosé
jelly mixture over and chill in the
refrigerator until the jelly is set.

■ Mix the lemon rind, remaining sugar
and 6 tablespoons wine together to make
a syllabub and set aside. When ready to
serve, whip the cream until it forms soft
swirls, then gradually whisk in the lemon
rind mixture. Spoon over the jellies.

TRY SOME FIZZ

For buck's fizz jellies, dissolve the gelatine as opposite, add 25 g (1 oz) caster sugar and when cool mix in 200 ml (7 fl oz) blood (or ordinary) orange juice and 500 ml (17 fl oz) cheap dry sparkling white wine. Divide 150 g (5 oz) fresh or frozen raspberries between the glasses, then top up with the jelly. Chill until set and serve plain.

SERVES 8-10

Preparation time 10 minutes, plus standing,
chilling & freezing
Cooking time 15 minutes

INGREDIENTS

1	**1 litre (1¾ pints) good-quality vanilla ice cream**
2	**250 g (8 oz) digestive biscuits, crushed**
3	**75 g (3 oz) butter, melted**
4	**200 g (7 oz) soft butterscotch fudge**
5	**2 tablespoons single cream**

Caramel Ice Cream Cake

■ Remove the ice cream from the freezer and leave to stand at room temperature for 30–45 minutes until it is well softened.

■ Meanwhile, put the crushed biscuits in a bowl, add the melted butter and mix together until the biscuits are moistened. Press the biscuit mixture into a 23 cm (9 inch) round springform tin, pressing it up the edge of the tin to give a 2.5 cm (1 inch) side. Chill in the refrigerator for 20 minutes.

■ Put the fudge and cream in a saucepan and heat gently, stirring, until the fudge has melted. Carefully spread two-thirds of the fudge mixture over the biscuit case. Spoon the ice cream over the top and level the surface.

■ Drizzle the remaining caramel over the ice cream with a spoon and freeze for 4 hours. Unmould the cake and serve in wedges.

ADD SOME CHOCOLATE

For a chocolate & caramel cake, make the biscuit case opposite, but use 250 g (8 oz) crushed chocolate digestive biscuits or chocolate cookies. Melt the fudge with the cream as above, then stir in 125 g (4 oz) toasted ground hazelnuts. Pour all the mixture into the biscuit base, then top with the softened vanilla ice cream. Melt 50 g (2 oz) plain dark chocolate in a heatproof bowl set over a saucepan of gently simmering water (don't let the bowl touch the water). Drizzle over the ice cream and freeze as opposite.

Preparation time 15 minutes
Cooking time 40 minutes

INGREDIENTS

1   **250 g (8 oz) plain dark chocolate, broken into pieces**

2   **125 g (4 oz) unsalted butter**

3   **50 ml (2 fl oz) double cream, plus an extra 50 ml (2 fl oz), whipped, to serve**

4   **4 eggs, separated**

5   **2 tablespoons cocoa powder, sifted**

STORECUPBOARD

125 g (4 oz) caster sugar

Chocolate Truffle Cake

■ Melt the chocolate, butter and cream together in a heatproof bowl set over a saucepan of gently simmering water. Remove from the heat and leave to cool for 5 minutes.

■ Whisk the egg yolks with 75 g (3 oz) of the caster sugar until pale and stir in the cooled chocolate mixture.

■ Whisk the egg whites in a large clean bowl until softly peaking then whisk in the remaining caster sugar. Fold into the egg yolk mixture with the sifted cocoa powder until evenly incorporated.

■ Pour the cake mixture into an oiled and base-lined 23 cm (9 inch) spring-form cake tin that has been lightly dusted all over with a little extra cocoa powder. Bake in a preheated oven, 180°C (350°F), Gas Mark 4, for 35 minutes.

■ Leave to cool in the tin for 10 minutes then turn out on to a serving plate. Serve in wedges, while still warm, with whipped cream and a few strawberries if liked.

TRY IT WITH ORANGE

For chocolate & brandied orange cake, add the finely grated rind of 1 orange when folding in the icing sugar opposite. Remove and discard the rind from 3 oranges, cut into segments and soak in 3 tablespoons brandy and 1 tablespoon clear honey. Serve the oranges with the cake and spoon over crème fraîche.

SERVES 8

Preparation time 20 minutes, plus chilling
and cooling
Cooking time 45–50 minutes

INGREDIENTS

 450 g (14½ oz) chilled ready-made or
homemade sweet shortcrust pastry

2 3 eggs plus 1 egg yolk

3 450 ml (¾ pint) double cream

STORECUPBOARD

100 g (3½ oz) caster sugar; 150 ml (¼ pint) lemon
juice; icing sugar, for dusting

Classic Lemon Tart

■ Roll out the pastry thinly on a lightly
floured surface and use it to line a 25 cm
(10 inch) fluted flan tin. Prick the pastry
shell with a fork and then chill in the
refrigerator for 15 minutes.

■ Line the pastry shell with nonstick
baking paper, add baking beans and bake
blind in a preheated oven, 190°C (375°F),
Gas Mark 5, for 15 minutes. Remove the
paper and beans and bake for a further
10 minutes until crisp and golden. Remove
from the oven and reduce the temperature
to 150°C (300°F), Gas Mark 2.

■ Beat together the eggs, egg yolk,
double cream, sugar and lemon juice, then
pour into the pastry shell.

■ Bake for 20–25 minutes or until the filling
is just set. Let the tart cool completely, then
dust with icing sugar and serve.

MAKE AN ACCOMPANIMENT

For mixed berries with cassis, to serve with the tart, halve or slice 250 g (8 oz) strawberries, depending on their size, and mix with 125 g (4 oz) raspberries, 125 g (4 oz) blueberries, 3 tablespoons caster sugar and 2 tablespoons crème de cassis. Soak for 1 hour before serving.

Preparation time 15 minutes, plus standing
Cooking time 1¼ hours

INGREDIENTS

1 5 chai tea bags

2 300 g (10 oz) mixed dried fruit

3 50 g (2 oz) Brazil nuts, chopped

4 50 g (2 oz) butter

5 1 egg, beaten

STORECUPBOARD

300 ml (½ pint) boiling water; 250 g (8 oz)
self-raising flour; 1 teaspoon baking powder;
150 g (5 oz) light muscovado sugar

Chai Teabread

■ Stir the tea bags into the measurement water in a jug and leave to stand for 10 minutes.

■ Grease a 1 kg (2 lb) or 1.3 litre (2¼ pint) loaf tin and line with parchment paper.

■ Mix together the flour, baking powder, sugar, dried fruit and nuts in a bowl. Remove the tea bags from the water, pressing them against the side of the jug to squeeze out all the water. Thinly slice the butter into the water and stir until melted. Leave to cool slightly. Add to the dry ingredients with the egg and mix together well.

■ Spoon the mixture into the prepared tin and spread the mixture into the corners. Bake in a preheated oven, 160°C (325°F), Gas Mark 3, for 1¼ hours or until risen, firm and a skewer inserted into the centre comes out clean.

■ Loosen the cake at the ends and transfer to a wire rack. Peel off the lining paper and leave to cool. Spread the top with Chai Cream Frosting, if liked (see opposite).

FROST THE CAKE

For chai cream frosting, to spread over the cake, put 50 ml (2 fl oz) milk and 3 chai tea bags in a saucepan and bring to the boil. Remove from the heat and leave the tea bags to infuse in the milk until cold. Discard the tea bags, squeezing them to extract the liquid. Beat together 200 g (7 oz) cream cheese and 25 g (1 oz) very soft unsalted butter in a bowl until smooth. Beat in the flavoured milk and 75 g (3 oz) sifted icing sugar.

SERVES 4

Preparation time 15 minutes
Cooking time none

INGREDIENTS

1	250 g (8 oz) fromage frais
2	100 g (3½ oz) sweetened chestnut purée
3	100 g (3½ oz) meringues, crushed
4	dark chocolate shards cut from a bar, to decorate

STORECUPBOARD

1 tablespoon icing sugar, sifted

Sweet Chestnut Mess

■ Beat the fromage frais with the icing sugar. Stir in half the chestnut purée and the crushed meringues.

■ Spoon the remaining chestnut purée into individual serving dishes and top with the meringue mess. Decorate with the dark chocolate shards and serve.

TRY IT WITH PANCAKES

For sweet chestnut pancakes, stir the chestnut purée into the fromage frais. Heat 8 ready-made pancakes according to the instructions on the packet and spread them with the chestnut purée mix. Roll them up and sprinkle with cocoa and icing sugar.

SERVES 4

Preparation time 10 minutes
Cooking time 20 minutes

INGREDIENTS

1	600 g (1 lb 3½ oz) dark chocolate
2	200 g (7 oz) milk chocolate
3	250 g (8 oz) mascarpone cheese
4	100 g (3½ oz) raspberries
5	finely chopped nuts, to decorate

Chocolate Millefeuilles

■ Break the dark and milk chocolate into pieces, place in separate heatproof bowls and melt over saucepans of barely simmering water, making sure the water does not touch the surface of the bowls.

■ Spread a thin layer of melted dark chocolate on to a sheet of baking parchment. Drizzle melted milk chocolate over the top and feather the 2 chocolates together. Leave until set but not brittle.

■ Cut into 7 cm (3 inch) squares, then leave until brittle before peeling away the paper.

■ Layer the chocolate rectangles with spoonfuls of mascarpone and raspberries and sprinkle with some nuts to decorate.

MAKE IT FRUITY

For raspberry millefeuilles, use 800 g (1 lb 10 oz) white chocolate to make the squares as opposite. Layer with cream and raspberries. Make a coulis by mixing 125 g (4 oz) fresh raspberries with 1 teaspoon icing sugar. Press the mixture through a sieve. Drizzle the coulis around the millefeuilles before serving.

Preparation time 15 minutes, plus cooling and chilling
Cooking time about 10 minutes

INGREDIENTS

1   50 g (2 oz) flaked almonds, toasted

2   200 ml (7 fl oz) coconut cream

3   300 ml (½ pint) double cream

4   15 cardamom seeds, lightly crushed

STORECUPBOARD

100 g (3½ oz) granulated sugar;
2 tablespoons caster sugar

Coconut Syllabub & Almond Brittle

■ To make the brittle, put the granulated sugar and flaked almonds in a saucepan over a low heat. While the sugar melts, lightly oil a baking sheet. When the sugar has melted and turned golden, pour the mixture on to the baking sheet and leave to cool.

■ To make the syllabub, pour the coconut cream and double cream into a large bowl. Add the crushed cardamom seeds and caster sugar, then lightly whip until just holding soft peaks.

■ Spoon the syllabub into 4 glasses and chill in the refrigerator. Meanwhile, lightly crack the brittle into irregular shards. When ready to serve, top the syllabub with some of the brittle and serve the remainder separately on the side.

SERVES 4

Preparation time 8 minutes
Cooking time none

INGREDIENTS

1   6 passion fruit, halved, flesh and seeds removed

2   300 ml (½ pint) Greek yogurt

3   1 tablespoon clear honey

4   200 ml (7 fl oz) whipping cream, whipped to soft peaks

5   4 pieces of shortbread, to serve

Passion Fruit Yogurt Fool

■ Stir the passion fruit flesh and seeds into the yogurt with the honey.

■ Fold the cream into the yogurt. Spoon into tall glasses and serve with the shortbread.

MIX UP THE FRUIT

For mango & lime yogurt fool, omit the passion fruit, instead puréeing 1 large ripe peeled and stoned mango with the zest of 1 lime and icing sugar to taste. Mix into the yogurt and fold in the cream. Omit the honey.

Preparation time 25 minutes
Cooking time 1 hour

INGREDIENTS

1   **225 g (7½ oz) ready-made puff pastry**

2   **175 g (6 oz) slightly salted butter, softened**

3   **3 eggs**

4   **6 figs, quartered**

STORECUPBOARD

175 g (6 oz) caster sugar; 200 g (7 oz) self-raising flour; ½ teaspoon baking powder; 100 g (3½ oz) icing sugar, sifted; 1 tablespoon lemon juice

Iced Fig Slice

■ Roll out the pastry on a lightly floured surface and use to line a greased 23 cm (9 inch) square shallow baking tin or small roasting tin. Line the pastry case with greaseproof paper and fill with baking beans (or dried beans reserved for the purpose). Bake in a preheated oven, 200°C (400°F), Gas Mark 6, for 15 minutes. Remove from the oven and remove the paper and beans. Reduce the oven temperature to 180°C (350°F), Gas Mark 4.

■ Beat together the butter, caster sugar, flour, baking powder and eggs in a bowl until pale and creamy. Spoon over the pastry base and level the surface. Arrange the figs over the top. Bake in the oven for about 45 minutes or until risen and golden. Leave to cool in the tin.

■ Make the icing. Beat together the icing sugar and lemon juice in a bowl to make a smooth, spoonable icing. If necessary, beat in a dash of water or extra lemon juice. Drizzle the icing over the cake, then cut into squares or fingers.

MAKES 8

Preparation time 30 minutes
Cooking time 10–12 minutes

INGREDIENTS

1   125 g (4 oz) butter, diced

2   1 tablespoon lavender petals

3   250 g (8 oz) strawberries (or a mixture of strawberries and raspberries)

4   150 ml (¼ pint) double cream

5   16 small lavender flowers (optional)

STORECUPBOARD

150 g (5 oz) plain flour; 25 g (1 oz) ground rice; 50 g (2 oz) caster sugar; sifted icing sugar, for dusting

Strawberry & Lavender Shortcakes

■ Put the flour and ground rice in a mixing bowl or a food processor. Add the butter and rub in with your fingertips or process until the mixture resembles fine breadcrumbs.

■ Stir in the sugar and lavender petals and squeeze the crumbs together with your hands to form a smooth ball. Knead lightly then roll out on a lightly floured surface until 5 mm (¼ inch) thick. Stamp out 7.5 cm (3 inch) circles using a fluted round biscuit cutter. Transfer to an ungreased baking sheet. Reknead the trimmings and continue rolling and stamping out until you have made 16 biscuits.

■ Prick with a fork, bake in a preheated oven, 160°C (325°F), Gas Mark 3, for 10–12 minutes until pale golden. Leave to cool on the baking tray.

■ To serve, halve 4 of the smallest strawberries, hull and slice the rest. Whip the cream and spoon over 8 of the biscuits. Top with the sliced strawberries then the remaining biscuits. Spoon the remaining cream on top and decorate with the reserved halved strawberries and tiny sprigs of lavender, if liked. Dust lightly with sifted icing sugar. These are best eaten on the day they are filled, but the plain biscuits can be stored in an airtight tin for up to 3 days.

Preparation time 15 minutes
Cooking time 20 minutes

INGREDIENTS

1   125 g (4 oz) lightly salted butter, softened

2   2 eggs

3   2 teaspoons espresso coffee powder

4   50 g (2 oz) flaked almonds, lightly toasted

5   ¼ teaspoon ground cinnamon

STORECUPBOARD

125 g (4 oz) caster sugar, plus 2 teaspoons;
150 g (5 oz) self-raising flour; ½ teaspoon baking
powder; 1 teaspoon boiling water

Marbled Coffee Cupcakes

■ Line a 12-section bun tin with paper cake cases.

■ Put the butter, 125 g (4 oz) caster sugar, eggs, flour and baking powder in a bowl and beat with a hand-held electric whisk for about a minute until light and creamy.

■ Spoon half the cake mixture into a separate bowl. Blend the coffee powder with the boiling water and stir into half the mixture. Using a teaspoon, fill the paper cases with the 2 mixtures, then draw a knife in a circular motion through each cupcake to mix the mixtures partially together to create a marbled effect.

■ Scatter the flaked almonds over the cakes. Mix the remaining 2 teaspoons sugar with the cinnamon and sprinkle over the cakes.

■ Bake in a preheated oven, 180°C (350°F), Gas Mark 4, for 20 minutes or until risen and just firm to the touch. Transfer to a wire rack to cool.

TRY A FRUITY CUPCAKE

For rippled raspberry cupcakes, make the cake mixture as opposite. Crush 75 g (3 oz) fresh raspberries in a bowl with 2 teaspoons caster sugar so that they are broken up but not turning to a juicy mush. Half fill the paper cases with the cake mixture and flatten with the back of a spoon. Divide the raspberry mixture between the cases and top with the remaining cake mixture. Bake as opposite and serve dusted with icing sugar.

FAMILY
FAVOURITES

Preparation time 10 minutes
Cooking time 5 minutes

INGREDIENTS

1   8 tablespoons shop-bought Belgian chocolate sauce

2   100 g (3 oz) chocolate chip cookies, broken into small pieces

3   16 small scoops of vanilla ice cream

4   200 g (7 oz) pink and white marshmallows, plus a few mini marshmallows, to decorate

5   grated chocolate, to decorate

Rocky Road Ice Cream Sundaes

■ Place the chocolate sauce in a saucepan over a low heat and warm through.

■ Meanwhile, place a handful of the cookies in each of 4 tall sundae glasses. Add 2 scoops of vanilla ice cream to each glass. Add 25 g (1 oz) of the marshmallows to each sundae, then spoon 1 tablespoon of the warm chocolate sauce over each. Repeat the layers, finishing with the chocolate sauce.

■ Decorate with a few mini marshmallows and a little grated chocolate. Serve immediately with long spoons.

MAKES 8

Preparation time 30 minutes
Cooking time 1–1¼ hours

INGREDIENTS

1	3 egg whites
2	1 small ripe banana
3	150 ml (¼ pint) double cream
4	8 tablespoons ready-made toffee fudge sauce

STORECUPBOARD

100 g (3½ oz) light muscovado sugar;
75 g (3 oz) caster sugar; 1 tablespoon lemon juice

Banoffee Meringues

■ Whisk the egg whites in a large clean bowl until stiff. Gradually whisk in the sugars, a teaspoonful at a time, until it has all been added. Whisk for a few minutes more until the meringue mixture is thick and glossy.

■ Using a dessertspoon, take a large scoop of meringue mixture then scoop off the first spoon using a second spoon and drop on to a large baking sheet lined with nonstick baking paper to make an oval-shaped meringue. Continue until all the mixture has been used.

■ Bake in a preheated oven, 110°C (225°F), Gas Mark ¼, for 1–1¼ hours or until the meringues are firm and may be easily peeled off the paper. Leave to cool still on the paper.

■ To serve, roughly mash the banana with the lemon juice. Whip the cream until it forms soft swirls, then whisk in 2 tablespoons of the toffee fudge sauce. Combine with the mashed banana then use to sandwich the meringues together in pairs and arrange in paper cake cases. Drizzle with the remaining toffee fudge sauce and serve immediately. Unfilled meringues may be stored in an airtight tin for up to 3 days.

TRY COFFEE TOFFEE

For coffee toffee meringues, make the meringues opposite. To make the filling, whip the cream, then stir in 1–2 teaspoons instant coffee, dissolved in 1 teaspoon boiling water. Use to sandwich the meringues together in pairs. Drizzle toffee fudge sauce over the top of the meringues.

SERVES 4

Preparation time 20 minutes
Cooking time 2 hours

INGREDIENTS

1	125 g (4 oz) unsalted butter
2	4 tablespoons golden syrup
3	2 cooking apples, about 500 g (1 lb) in total, cored and peeled
4	2 eggs, beaten
5	grated rind of 1 orange, and 3 tablespoons of the juice

STORECUPBOARD

100 g (3½ oz) caster sugar;
200 g (7 oz) self-raising flour

Steamed Apple Pudding

■ Grease the inside of a 1.2 litre (2 pint) pudding basin lightly and line the base with a small circle of nonstick baking paper. Spoon in the syrup, then thickly slice 1 apple and arrange in an even layer on top. Coarsely grate the remaining apple.

■ Cream the butter and sugar in a bowl until pale and creamy. Gradually mix in alternate spoonfuls of beaten egg and flour until both have all been added and the mixture is smooth.

■ Stir in the grated apple, orange rind and juice, then spoon into the pudding basin. Level the surface and cover with a piece of pleated nonstick baking paper and foil. Tie in place with string, adding a string handle.

■ Lower the basin into the top of a steamer set over a saucepan of simmering water, cover with a lid and steam for 2 hours until the pudding is well risen and a knife comes out cleanly when inserted into the centre of the sponge.

■ Remove the foil and paper, loosen the edge of the pudding and turn out on to a plate with a rim. Serve immediately.

CUTS INTO 10

Preparation time 25 minutes
Cooking time 1 hour–1 hour 10 minutes

INGREDIENTS

1	175 g (6 oz) butter, at room temperature

2	3 eggs, beaten

3	40 g (1½ oz) poppy seeds

4	citron peel, cut into thin strips

STORECUPBOARD

175 g (6 oz) caster sugar; 250 g (8 oz) self-raising flour; 1 teaspoon baking powder; grated rind and juice of 2 lemons, 125 g (4 oz) icing sugar

Lemon & Poppy Seed Cake

■ Beat the butter and caster sugar together in a mixing bowl until pale and creamy. Gradually mix in alternate spoonfuls of beaten egg and flour until all has been added and the mixture is smooth. Stir in the baking powder, poppy seeds, lemon rind and 5–6 tablespoons lemon juice to make a soft dropping consistency, Ensure you reserve about 3 teaspoons of lemon juice for the icing.

■ Spoon the mixture into a greased 1 kg (2 lb) loaf tin, its base and 2 long sides also lined with oiled greaseproof paper. Spread the surface level and bake in a preheated oven, 160°C (325°F), Gas Mark 3, for 1 hour–1 hour 10 minutes until well risen, the top is cracked and golden and a skewer inserted into the centre comes out clean.

■ Leave to cool in the tin for 10 minutes then loosen the edges and lift out of the tin using the lining paper. Transfer to a wire rack, peel off the lining paper and leave to cool.

■ Sift the icing sugar into a bowl then gradually mix in enough of the lemon juice to make a smooth coating icing. Drizzle over the top of the cake in random squiggly lines. Add strips of citron peel to the top and leave to set. Store in an airtight tin for up to 1 week.

CUTS INTO 8

Preparation time 30 minutes
Cooking time 20 minutes

INGREDIENTS

| 1 | 175 g (6 oz) soft margarine |

| 2 | 3 eggs |

| 3 | 6 teaspoons instant coffee, dissolved in 3 teaspoons boiling water |

| 4 | 75 g (3 oz) butter, at room temperature |

| 5 | 50 g (2 oz) dark chocolate, melted, for drizzling |

STORECUPBOARD

175 g (6 oz) light muscovado sugar; 175 g (6 oz) self-raising flour; 1 teaspoon baking powder; 150 g (5 oz) icing sugar, sifted

Old-fashioned Coffee Cake

■ Beat together the margarine, muscovado sugar, flour, baking powder, eggs and half the dissolved coffee in a mixing bowl or a food processor until smooth.

■ Divide the mixture evenly between 2 × 18 cm (7 inch) sandwich tins, greased and base-lined with oiled greaseproof paper, and spread the surfaces level. Bake in a preheated oven, 180°C (350°F), Gas Mark 4, for 20 minutes until well risen, the cakes are browned and spring back when gently pressed with a fingertip.

■ Leave the cakes for a few minutes then loosen the edges, turn out on to a wire rack and peel off the lining paper. Leave to cool.

■ Next make the coffee frosting. Put the butter and half the icing sugar in a mixing bowl, add the remaining dissolved coffee and beat until smooth. Gradually beat in the remaining icing sugar until pale and creamy.

■ Put one of the cakes on a serving plate, spread with half the frosting then cover with the second cake. Spread the remaining frosting over the top.

■ Pipe or drizzle swirls of melted chocolate on top. This cake can be stored in a cake tin for 2–3 days in a cool place.

MAKES 12

Preparation time 20 minutes
Cooking time 6–9 minutes

INGREDIENTS

1   1 egg, beaten plus 1 egg yolk

2   1 teaspoon vanilla essence

3   1 teaspoon ground cinnamon

STORECUPBOARD

200 g (7 oz) plain flour; ¼ teaspoon salt;
5 tablespoons caster sugar; 275 ml (9 fl oz) water;
1 litre (1¾ pints) sunflower oil

Churros

■ Mix the flour, salt and 1 tablespoon of the sugar in a bowl. Pour the water into a saucepan and bring to the boil. Take off the heat, add the flour mixture and beat well. Then return to the heat and stir until it forms a smooth ball that leaves the sides of the pan almost clean. Remove from the heat and leave to cool for 10 minutes.

■ Gradually beat the whole egg, egg yolk then the vanilla essence into the flour mixture until smooth. Spoon into a large nylon piping bag fitted with a 1 cm (½ inch) wide plain tube.

■ Pour the oil into a medium-sized saucepan to a depth of 2.5 cm (1 inch). Heat to 170°C (340°F) on a sugar thermometer or pipe a tiny amount of the mixture into the oil. If the oil bubbles instantly it is ready to use. Pipe coils, S-shapes and squiggly lines into the oil,

in small batches, cutting the ends off with kitchen scissors. Cook the churros for 2–3 minutes until they float and are golden, turning over if needed to brown evenly.

■ Lift the churros out of the oil, drain well on kitchen paper then sprinkle with the remaining sugar mixed with the cinnamon. Continue piping and frying until all the mixture has been used. Serve warm or cold.

■ These are best eaten on the day they are made.

ADD CITRUS

For orange churros, add the grated rind of 1 orange and omit the vanilla essence. Continue as opposite. Sprinkle with plain caster sugar when cooked.

SERVES 6

Preparation time 40 minutes, plus cooling
Cooking time 30–35 minutes

INGREDIENTS

1   **470 g (15 oz) ready-made or homemade all-butter sweet shortcrust pastry**

2   **750 g (1½ lb) peaches, halved, stoned, sliced**

3   **150 g (5 oz) raspberries**

4   **milk, to glaze**

STORECUPBOARD

75 g (3 oz) caster sugar, plus extra for sprinkling; 1 teaspoon cornflour; grated rind of 1 lemon

Peach Melba Pie

■ Reserve one-third of the pastry for the lattice. Roll out the remainder on a lightly floured surface until large enough to line the base and sides of a buttered metal pie dish, 20 cm (8 inches) in diameter and 5 cm (2 inches) deep. Lift the pastry over a rolling pin, drape into the dish, then press over the base and sides.

■ Mix the sugar, cornflour and lemon rind together, then add the fruits and toss together gently. Pile into the pie dish. Trim off the excess pastry, add to the reserved portion, then roll out. Cut into 1.5 cm (¾ inch) wide strips long enough to go over the top of the pie.

■ Brush the top edge of the pie with milk and arrange the pastry strips over the top as a lattice. Trim off the excess. Brush with milk, then sprinkle with a little sugar.

■ Bake in a preheated oven, 190°C (375°F), Gas Mark 5, for 30–35 minutes until golden. Leave to cool for 15 minutes, then serve cut into wedges and drizzled with melba sauce (see opposite).

A SAUCEY EXTRA

For melba sauce, to serve as an accompaniment, put 200 g (7 oz) raspberries in a saucepan with the juice of ½ lemon and 2 tablespoons icing sugar, and cook for 2–3 minutes until the raspberries are just tender. Cool, then purée in a blender and sieve to remove the seeds. Serve warm or cold.

Preparation time 15 minutes
Cooking time 16–20 minutes

INGREDIENTS

1 ½ **teaspoon ground cinnamon**

2 ½ **teaspoon ground ginger**

3 ¼ **teaspoon ground allspice or mixed spice**

4 50 g (2 oz) butter, diced

5 2 tablespoons golden syrup

STORECUPBOARD

100 g (3½ oz) plain flour; 1 teaspoon baking powder; ½ teaspoon bicarbonate of soda; finely grated rind of 1 lemon; 50 g (2 oz) caster sugar

Fairings

■ Mix the flour, baking powder, bicarbonate of soda, spices and lemon rind together in a mixing bowl.

■ Add the butter and rub in with your fingertips until the mixture resembles fine breadcrumbs.

■ Stir in the sugar, add the syrup, then mix together first with a spoon then squeeze the crumbs together with your hands to form a ball.

■ Shape the dough into a log then slice into 12. Roll each piece into a ball and arrange on 2 large greased baking sheets, leaving space between for them to spread during cooking.

■ Cook one baking sheet at a time in the centre of a preheated oven, 180°C (350°F), Gas Mark 4, for 8–10 minutes or until the biscuit tops are cracked and golden.

■ Leave to harden for 1–2 minutes, then loosen and transfer to a wire rack to cool completely. Store in an airtight tin for up to 3 days.

Preparation time 15 minutes, plus freezing time
Cooking time 5 minutes

INGREDIENTS

1 4 slices jam Swiss roll or 4 trifle sponges, separated, with the corners trimmed off

2 4 scoops strawberry and vanilla ice cream or vanilla ice cream

3 2 egg whites

4 175 g (6 oz) frozen summer fruits, just defrosted or warmed in a small saucepan

STORECUPBOARD

50 g (2 oz) caster sugar

Mini Baked Alaskas

■ Arrange the slices of Swiss roll or trifle sponge, well spaced apart, on a baking sheet, then top each with a scoop of ice cream. Put into the freezer for 10 minutes (or longer if you have time).

■ Whisk the egg whites in a large bowl until stiff, moist-looking peaks form. Gradually whisk in the sugar, a teaspoon at a time, and continue whisking for a few minutes until thick and glossy.

■ Take the sponge and ice cream from the freezer and quickly swirl the meringue over the top and sides to cover completely. Cook in a preheated oven, 200°C (400°F), Gas Mark 6, for 5 minutes until the peaks are golden brown, the meringue is cooked through and the ice cream is only just beginning to soften.

■ Transfer the baked Alaskas to shallow serving bowls and spoon the summer fruit around the base of the desserts. Serve immediately.

TRY A COFFEE ALTERNATIVE

For cappuccino Alaskas, use chocolate Swiss roll (choose one without a chocolate outside coating) instead of the jam Swiss roll or trifle sponges. Top each slice with a scoop of coffee ice cream, then the meringue as opposite. When baked, dust lightly with sifted drinking chocolate powder and serve.

Preparation time 10 minutes
Cooking time 12 minutes

INGREDIENTS

1 125 g (4 oz) unsalted butter, at room temperature

2 125 g (4 oz) chunky peanut butter

3 1 egg, lightly beaten

4 125 g (4 oz) unsalted peanuts

STORECUPBOARD

150 g (5 oz) soft brown sugar; 150 g (5 oz) plain flour; ½ teaspoon baking powder

Peanut Butter Cookies

■ Beat the butter and sugar together in a mixing bowl or a food processor until pale and creamy. Add the peanut butter, egg, flour and baking powder and stir together until combined. Stir in the peanuts.

■ Drop large teaspoonfuls of the mixture on to 3 large, lightly oiled baking sheets, leaving 5 cm (2 inch) gaps between each for them to spread during cooking.

■ Flatten the mounds slightly and bake in a preheated oven, 190°C (375°F), Gas Mark 5, for 12 minutes until golden around the edges. Leave to cool on the baking sheets for 2 minutes then transfer to a wire rack to cool completely.

ADD CHOCOLATE CHIPS

For peanut butter & chocolate chip cookies, use only 50 g (2 oz) unsalted peanuts and add 50 g (2 oz) milk chocolate chips. Then make and bake the cookies as opposite.

Preparation time 7 minutes
Cooking time 15 minutes

INGREDIENTS

1 1 kg (2 lb) Bramley apples, peeled, cored and thickly sliced

2 75 g (3 oz) butter

3 75 g (3 oz) fresh wholemeal breadcrumbs

4 25 g (1 oz) pumpkin seeds

STORECUPBOARD

2 tablespoons caster sugar, 1 tablespoon lemon juice;
2 tablespoons water; 2 tablespoons soft brown sugar

Instant Apple Crumbles

■ Place the apples in a saucepan with 25 g (1 oz) butter, the caster sugar, lemon juice and measurement water. Cover and simmer for 8–10 minutes, until softened.

■ Make a crumble by melting the remaining butter in a frying pan, add the breadcrumbs and stir-fry until lightly golden, then add the pumpkin seeds and stir-fry for a further 1 minute. Remove from the heat and stir in the brown sugar.

■ Spoon the apple mixture into bowls, sprinkle with the crumble and serve.

CHANGE THE FRUIT

For instant pear & chocolate crumble, cook 1 kg (2 lb) pears in the butter, sugar and water as in the recipe opposite, adding ½ teaspoon ground ginger to the butter. Prepare the crumble opposite, replacing the pumpkin seeds with 50 g (2 oz) roughly chopped plain chocolate. Cook as opposite.

INGREDIENTS

1   8 sponge fingers or 100 g (3½ oz) plain sponge or jam-filled Swiss roll

2   3 tablespoons orange juice

3   375 g (12 oz) frozen mixed summer fruits, just thawed

4   425 g (14 oz) ready-made custard

5   3 egg whites

STORECUPBOARD

75 g (3 oz) granulated sugar

Warm Summer Fruit Trifle

■ Crumble the sponge fingers or cake into the bottom of 6 individual ovenproof dishes. Drizzle the orange juice over the tops, then add the mixed fruits. Dollop the custard over the tops.

■ Whisk the egg whites in a clean, dry bowl until stiff peaks form, then gradually whisk in the sugar, a spoonful at a time, until all the sugar has been added. Keep whisking for another 1–2 minutes until the mixture is thick and glossy.

■ Spoon the meringue mixture over the top of the custard in large swirls. Place the dishes on a baking sheet. Cook in a preheated oven, 160°C (325°F), Gas Mark 3, for 20 minutes until the meringue is golden brown on top. Serve warm.

MAKE IT SUMMERY

For chilled summer fruit trifle, in the bottom of a large bowl, sprinkle the crumbled sponge finger biscuits or cake with 3 tablespoons sherry. Top with the thawed fruits, then the custard. Whip 150 ml (¼ pint) double cream until it forms soft swirls. Spoon over the top of the trifle instead of the meringue. Chill until ready to serve, then decorate with sugar sprinkles or 4 teaspoons toasted flaked almonds.

SERVES 6

Preparation time 40 minutes, plus chilling and standing
Cooking time 35–40 minutes

INGREDIENTS

 375 g (12 oz) chilled ready-made or homemade sweet shortcrust pastry

 4 eggs, separated

STORECUPBOARD

a little flour, for dusting, 200 g (7 oz) caster sugar, 40 g (1½ oz) cornflour; grated rind and juice of 2 lemons; 200–250 ml (7–8 fl oz) water

Lemon Meringue Pie

■ Roll out the pastry thinly on a lightly floured surface and use to line a 20 cm (8 inch) diameter × 5 cm (2 inch) deep loose-bottomed fluted flan tin, pressing evenly into the sides. Trim the top and prick the base. Chill for 15 minutes, then line with nonstick baking paper, add baking beans and bake blind in a preheated oven, 190°C (375°F), Gas Mark 5, for 15 minutes. Remove the paper and beans and bake for a further 5 minutes.

■ Put 75 g (3 oz) of the sugar in a bowl with the cornflour and lemon rind, add the egg yolks and mix until smooth. Make the lemon juice up to 300 ml (½ pint) with water, pour into a saucepan and bring to the boil. Gradually mix into the yolk mixture, whisking until smooth. Pour back into the pan and bring to the boil, whisking until very thick. Pour into the pastry case and spread level.

■ Whisk the egg whites until they form stiff peaks. Gradually whisk in the remaining sugar, a teaspoonful at a time, then whisk for 1–2 minutes more until thick and glossy. Spoon over the lemon layer to cover completely and swirl with a spoon.

■ Reduce the oven to 180°C (350°F), Gas Mark 4, and cook for 15–20 minutes until the meringue is golden and cooked through. Leave to stand for 15 minutes, then remove the tart tin and transfer to a serving plate. Serve warm or cold.

ADD MORE CITRUS

For citrus meringue pie, mix the grated rind of 1 lime, 1 lemon and ½ small orange with the cornflour. Squeeze the juice from the fruits and make up to 300 ml (½ pint) with water. Continue as opposite.

Preparation time 15 minutes
Cooking time 1¼ hours

INGREDIENTS

1	40 g (1½ oz) fresh raspberries, plus extra to serve (optional)
2	2 tablespoons raspberry jam
3	4 egg whites

STORECUPBOARD

200 g (7 oz) caster sugar

Raspberry Ripple Meringues

■ Put the raspberries in a bowl and mash with a fork until broken up and turning juicy. Add the jam and mash together to make a purée. Tip into a sieve resting over a small bowl and press the purée with the back of a spoon to extract as much juice as possible.

■ Whisk the egg whites in a large clean bowl with a hand-held electric whisk until peaking. Whisk in a tablespoonful of the sugar and continue to whisk for about 15 seconds. Gradually add the remaining sugar, a spoonful at a time, until thick and glossy.

■ Drizzle over the raspberry purée and lightly stir in using a spatula or large metal spoon, scooping up the meringue from the base of the bowl so that the mixture is streaked with the purée. Take care not to over-mix.

■ Drop large spoonfuls of the mixture, each about the size of a small orange, on to a large baking sheet lined with baking parchment, then swirl with the back of a teaspoon. Bake in a preheated oven, 120°C (250°F), Gas Mark ½, for about 1¼ hours or until the meringues are crisp and come away easily from the paper. Leave to cool on the paper. Serve with extra raspberries, if liked.

Preparation time 20 minutes
Cooking time 35 minutes

INGREDIENTS

 400 g (13 oz) plain dark chocolate

 175 g (6 oz) slightly salted butter

 3 eggs

STORECUPBOARD

225 g (7½ oz) light muscovado sugar;
100 g (3½ oz) self-raising flour

Rich Chocolate Brownies

■ Chop 150 g (5 oz) of the chocolate into 5 mm (¼ inch) pieces. Break the remaining chocolate into pieces and put in a heatproof bowl with the butter. Melt over a saucepan of gently simmering water (don't let the base of the bowl touch the water).

■ Beat the eggs and sugar in a separate bowl until light and foamy. Stir in the melted chocolate mixture. Tip in the flour and chopped chocolate and mix together until just combined.

■ Spoon the mixture into a greased and lined 28 × 18 cm (11 × 7 inch) shallow baking tin or roasting tin and level the surface. Bake in a preheated oven, 190°C (375°F), Gas Mark 5, for about 30 minutes or until a crust has formed but the mixture feels quite soft underneath. Leave to cool in the tin, then transfer to a board and cut into small squares. Peel off the lining paper.

SERVES 4

Preparation time 5 minutes
Cooking time none

FIVE INGREDIENTS

1   400 g (13 oz) frozen mixed summer berries

2   250 g (8 oz) fat-free Greek yogurt

3   wafers, to serve (optional)

STORECUPBOARD

2 tablespoons icing sugar

Frozen Berry Yogurt Ice Cream

■ Place half the berries, the yogurt and icing sugar in a food processor or blender and blend until fairly smooth and the berries have broken up.

■ Add the rest of the berries and pulse until they are slightly broken up but some texture remains.

■ Place scoops of the yogurt ice cream into bowls and serve immediately with wafers, if liked.

TRY IT IN A SUNDAE

Place 150 g (5 oz) raspberries and 1 tablespoon icing sugar in a food processor or blender and blend to make a smooth coulis, then sieve to remove the pips. Make the yogurt ice cream opposite. Break up 4 meringue nests and divide half between 4 glasses. Add 1 scoop of the yogurt ice cream to each glass, then pour over a little of the coulis. Repeat the layers, finishing with the coulis. Serve immediately.

Preparation time 20 minutes, plus cooling
Cooking time 1 hour 25 minutes

INGREDIENTS

1 250 g (8 oz) stoned dates, roughly chopped

2 2 small very ripe bananas

3 150 g (5 oz) slightly salted butter, softened

4 2 eggs

5 100 ml (3½ fl oz) milk

STORECUPBOARD

finely grated rind and juice of 1 lemon; 100 ml (3½ fl oz) water; 150 g (5 oz) caster sugar; 275 g (9 oz) self-raising flour; 1 teaspoon baking powder

Date & Banana Ripple Slice

■ Put 200 g (7 oz) of the dates in a small saucepan with the lemon rind and juice and measurement water. Bring to the boil, then reduce the heat and simmer gently for 5 minutes until the dates are soft and pulpy. Mash the mixture with a fork until fairly smooth. Leave to cool.

■ Grease a 1.25 kg (2½ lb) or 1.5 litre (2½ pint) loaf tin and line with nonstick baking paper.

■ Mash the bananas to a purée in a bowl, then add the butter, sugar, eggs, milk, flour and baking powder and beat together until smooth.

■ Spoon a third of the mixture into the prepared tin and level the surface. Spoon over half the date purée and spread evenly. Add half the remaining cake mixture and spread with the remaining purée. Add the remaining cake mixture and level the surface.

■ Scatter with the reserved dates and bake in a preheated oven, 160°C (325°F), Gas Mark 3, for about 1 hour 20 minutes or until risen and a skewer inserted into the centre comes out clean. Leave to cool in the tin for 15 minutes, then loosen at the ends and transfer to a wire rack. Peel off the lining paper and leave the cake to cool completely.

MINI BITES

MAKES 24

Preparation time 30 minutes,
plus chilling and cooling
Cooking time 11–13 minutes

INGREDIENTS

 1   375 g (12 oz) ready-made or homemade sweet shortcrust pastry, chilled

2   300 g (10 oz) blueberries

3   milk, to glaze

STORECUPBOARD

2 teaspoons cornflour; 3 teaspoons water;
40 g (1½ oz) caster sugar, plus extra for sprinkling

Blueberry Tarts

■ Roll the pastry out thinly on a lightly floured surface, then stamp out 24 × 6 cm (2½ inch) circles with a fluted biscuit cutter and press into the buttered sections of 2 × 12-section mini muffin tins, reserving any trimmings. Prick the base of each tart 2–3 times with a fork, then chill for 15 minutes.

■ Meanwhile, mix the cornflour and measurement water to a paste in a saucepan, then add the sugar and half the blueberries. Cook over a medium heat for 2–3 minutes until the blueberries soften and the juices begin to run. Take off the heat and add the remaining blueberries. Leave to cool.

■ Roll out the remaining pastry trimmings and cut out 24 tiny heart shapes. Place the heart shapes on a baking sheet, brush with milk and sprinkle with caster sugar.

■ Line the tarts with small squares of nonstick baking paper and baking beans and bake in a preheated oven, 190°C (375°F), Gas Mark 5, for 5 minutes. Remove the paper and beans from the tarts and cook for a further 4–5 minutes until the bases are crisp, cooking the heart shapes for 4–5 minutes on the shelf below.

■ Transfer the tart cases to a wire rack to cool. When ready to serve, spoon in the blueberry compote and top with the heart shapes.

TRY STRAWBERRY JAM

For mini jam tarts, make up the tart cases and decorations opposite. Spoon in 200 g (7 oz) strawberry jam, add the pastry shapes, then bake at 180°C (350°F), Gas Mark 4, for 12–15 minutes. Leave the tarts to cool for 5 minutes, then transfer to a wire rack to cool.

MAKES 24

Preparation time 15 minutes
Cooking time 8 minutes

INGREDIENTS

1 50 g (2 oz) sweetened dessicated coconut, plus 3 tablespoons for sprinkling

2 50 g (2 oz) white chocolate chips

3 150 ml (¼ pint) vanilla yogurt

4 1 egg

5 3 tablespoons strawberry jam

STORECUPBOARD

150 g (5 oz) self-raising flour; ½ teaspoon bicarbonate of soda; 75 g (3 oz) golden caster sugar; 4 tablespoons sunflower oil

White Chocolate Coconut Muffins

■ Line 2 × 12-hole mini muffin tins with paper cases.

■ Sift the flour and bicarbonate of soda into a bowl and add the sugar, coconut and white chocolate chips.

■ Mix the yogurt, egg and sunflower oil together and add to the dry ingredients. Using a large metal spoon, stir the ingredients together until just combined. Divide among the cases.

■ Bake in a preheated oven, 190°C (375°F), Gas Mark 5, for 6–8 minutes until the muffins are well risen and firm. Transfer to a wire rack.

■ Brush with the strawberry jam while the muffins are still warm, and sprinkle over the remaining coconut.

MAKES 12

Preparation time 20 minutes, plus cooling
Cooking time 20–25 minutes

INGREDIENTS

1   **150 g (5 oz) lightly salted butter, softened**

2   **3 eggs**

3   **1 teaspoon vanilla extract**

4   **4 passion fruit**

5   **150 ml (¼ pint) double cream**

STORECUPBOARD

150 g (5 oz) caster sugar; 150 g (5 oz) self-raising
flour; ½ teaspoon baking powder; 100–150 g
(3½–5 oz) icing sugar, plus 1 tablespoon

Passion Fruit Cream Cupcakes

■ Line a 12-section muffin tray with paper
muffin cases. Put the butter, caster sugar,
eggs, flour, baking powder and vanilla
extract in a bowl and beat with an electric
hand whisk for about a minute until light
and creamy. Divide the mixture between
the paper cases.

■ Bake in a preheated oven, 180°C
(350°F), Gas Mark 4, for 20–25 minutes
or until risen and just firm to the touch.
Transfer to a wire rack to cool.

■ Halve 2 of the passion fruit and scoop
the pulp into a bowl with the cream and
1 tablespoon of the icing sugar. Whip until
the cream only just holds its shape.

■ Peel away the cases from the cakes
and split each cake in half horizontally.
Sandwich the halves together with the
passion fruit cream.

■ Scoop the pulp of the remaining
2 passion fruit into a bowl. Gradually beat
in the remaining icing sugar until you have
a thin icing and spread over the cakes.

CHANGE THE FRUITS

For peach & redcurrant cupcakes, make and bake the cakes as opposite. Leave to cool and split horizontally. Whip 150 ml (¼ pint) double cream with 1 tablespoon orange-flavoured liqueur or orange juice and spoon over the bottom halves of the cakes. Pile 1 thinly sliced stoned ripe peach and 75 g (3 oz) redcurrants on top, then add the lids. Dust generously with icing sugar.

MAKES 16

Preparation time 15 minutes, plus cooling
Cooking time 10 minutes

INGREDIENTS

1   40 g (1½ oz) amaretti biscuits

2   65 g (2½ oz) lightly salted butter, softened

3   1 egg

4   4 plums, stoned and chopped

5   8 unblanched almonds, chopped

STORECUPBOARD

40 g (1½ oz) light muscovado sugar; 65 g (2½ oz)
self-raising flour; ½ teaspoon baking powder;
50 g (2 oz) icing sugar, sifted; 2 teaspoons lemon juice

Amaretti Plum Cakes

■ Place 16 mini silicone muffin cases on
a baking sheet.

■ Put the biscuits in a polythene bag and
crush with a rolling pin until finely ground.
Tip into a bowl and add the sugar, butter
and egg, then sift in the flour and baking
powder. Beat with a hand-held electric
whisk until smooth and creamy. Divide
among the cases.

■ Bake in a preheated oven, 180°C (350°F),
Gas Mark 4, for 10 minutes, or until risen and
just firm. Leave in the cases for 2 minutes,
then transfer to a wire rack to cool completely.

■ Make the icing by beating the icing sugar
with the lemon juice to make a smooth
paste. Spread a little over the cakes and
sprinkle over pieces of the chopped plums
and almonds. Drizzle a little more icing
on top.

SERVES 4

Preparation time 15 minutes
Cooking time 20–25 minutes

INGREDIENTS

1 375 g (12 oz) ready-rolled puff pastry, defrosted if frozen

2 100 g (3½ oz) marzipan

3 12 canned apricot halves, drained

4 apricot jam, to glaze

STORECUPBOARD

light muscovado sugar, for sprinkling

Apricot Tartlets

■ Cut 4 circles from the pastry using a saucer as a template, each approximately 8 cm (3½ inches) in diameter. Score a line about 1 cm (½ inch) from the edge of each circle with a sharp knife.

■ Roll out the marzipan to 5 mm (¼ inch) thick and cut out 4 rounds to fit inside the scored circles. Lay the pastry rounds on a baking sheet, place a circle of marzipan in the centre of each and arrange 3 apricot halves, cut-side up, on top. Sprinkle a little sugar into each apricot.

■ Put the baking sheet on top of a second preheated baking sheet (this helps to crisp the pastry bases) and bake in a preheated oven, 200°C (400°F), Gas Mark 6, for 20–25 minutes until the pastry is puffed and browned and the apricots are slightly caramelized around the edges. While still hot, brush the tops with apricot jam to glaze, then serve.

A JAMAICAN FLAVOUR

For banana tartlets with rum mascarpone, follow the recipe opposite, but use 2 thickly sliced bananas in place of the apricots. While the tartlets are baking, in a bowl, mix together 4 tablespoons mascarpone cheese, 2 tablespoons rum and 2 tablespoons light muscovado sugar. Spoon on top of the hot tartlets, then serve.

MAKES 12

Preparation time 30 minutes
Cooking time 35–40 minutes

INGREDIENTS

1 500 g (1 lb) ready-made puff pastry

2 3 eggs plus 2 egg yolks

3 1 teaspoon vanilla bean paste or extract

4 300 ml (½ pint) single cream

STORECUPBOARD

1 tablespoon vanilla sugar; 75 g (3 oz) caster sugar;
sifted icing sugar, for dusting

Mini Custard Tarts

■ Roll out the pastry on a floured surface to 5 mm (¼ inch) thick. Cut in half and sprinkle one half with the vanilla sugar. Lay the second piece on top and thinly roll out the pastry. Cut out 12 rounds using a 9 cm (3¾ inch) plain biscuit cutter. Re-roll the trimmings to make more.

■ Press the rounds into the holes of a 12-hole nonstick muffin tray, pressing firmly into the sections. Line the pastry cases with squares of foil. (To do this, wrap each foil square tightly around half a lemon, then remove. Press the foil domes firmly into the pastry cases.)

■ Bake in a preheated oven, 200°C (400°F), Gas Mark 6, for 15 minutes. Remove the foil and bake the cases for a further 5 minutes until crisp. Reduce the oven temperature to 160°C (325°F), Gas Mark 3.

■ Meanwhile, beat together the eggs, egg yolks, caster sugar and vanilla in a heatproof bowl. Bring the cream to the boil in a saucepan and pour over the egg mixture, whisking well. Strain into a jug and pour into the cases. Bake in the oven for 15–20 minutes or until just set and still slightly wobbly in the centre. Leave to cool in the tin. Serve dusted with sifted icing sugar.

SWAP CUSTARD FOR TREACLE

For lemon & treacle tarts, make and bake the pastry cases as opposite, omitting the vanilla sugar. Heat 400 g (13 oz) golden syrup in a saucepan until slightly thinned. Remove from the heat and beat in 75 g (3 oz) fresh white breadcrumbs, the finely grated rind of 2 lemons and 3 tablespoons lemon juice. Cool slightly, then beat in 1 egg and 1 egg yolk. Divide between the cases and return to the oven for 15 minutes until lightly set.

MAKES 12

Preparation time 15 minutes
Cooking time 25 minutes

INGREDIENTS

1	125 g (4 oz) lightly salted butter, softened
2	2 eggs
3	1 teaspoon vanilla extract
4	100 g (3½ oz) pecan nuts, roughly chopped
5	250 g (8 oz) caramel sauce

STORECUPBOARD

125 g (4 oz) light muscovado sugar; 150 g (5 oz)
self-raising flour; ½ teaspoon baking powder

Warm Pecan Caramel Cupcakes

■ Line a 12-section bun tin with paper cake
cases. Put the butter, sugar, eggs, flour,
baking powder and vanilla extract in a bowl
and beat with a hand-held electric whisk
for about a minute until light and creamy.

■ Stir in three-quarters of the pecan nuts
and then divide the cake mixture between
the paper cases.

■ Bake in a preheated oven, 180°C (350°F),
Gas Mark 4, for 20 minutes or until risen
and just firm to the touch. Transfer to a
wire rack.

■ Tip the caramel sauce into a small
saucepan and stir gently over a medium
heat until melted but not boiling. Drizzle
the sauce over the cakes while still warm
and scatter with the remaining pecan nuts.
You may want to take the cakes out of
their cases to serve.

Preparation time 25 minutes, plus cooling
Cooking time 12 minutes

INGREDIENTS

1 65 g (2½ oz) lightly salted butter, softened

2 1 teaspoon vanilla extract

3 1 egg

4 75 g (3 oz) unsalted butter, softened

5 pink food colouring

STORECUPBOARD

65 g (2½ oz) caster sugar; 65 g (2½ oz) self-raising
flour, sifted; icing sugar, for dusting; 100 g (3½ oz)
icing sugar, sifted; 1 teaspoon hot water

Baby Butterflies

■ Place 16 mini silicone muffin cases on
a baking sheet.

■ Put the salted butter, caster sugar, flour,
vanilla extract and egg in a bowl and beat
with a hand-held electric whisk until light
and creamy. Divide among the cases.

■ Bake in a preheated oven, 180°C (350°F),
Gas Mark 4, for 10–12 minutes until risen
and just firm. Leave to cool in the cases for
2 minutes then transfer to a wire rack to
cool completely.

■ Make the buttercream by beating
together the unsalted butter and icing
sugar until combined. Add a little pink food
colouring and the measurement water and
beat until smooth and creamy.

■ Use a small, sharp knife to cut out circles
from the tops of the cakes and cut the
circles in half to shape butterfly wings.

■ Put the buttercream in a piping bag
fitted with a small star nozzle and use to
pipe swirls into the scooped-out tops of
the cakes. Position the butterfly wings
on top and dust lightly with icing sugar.

ADD A FROSTING

For white chocolate frosting, melt 100 g (3½ oz) chopped white chocolate with 25 g (1 oz) unsalted butter in a microwave until no lumps remain. Remove from the heat and sift in 100 g (3½ oz) icing sugar. Stir well until combined. Use instead of the buttercream to spoon or pipe onto the cupcakes.

MAKES 16

Preparation time 15 minutes, plus cooling
Cooking time 20 minutes

INGREDIENTS

1 200 g (7 oz) unsalted butter, softened

2 1 teaspoon vanilla extract

3 3 tablespoons raspberry or strawberry jam

STORECUPBOARD

50 g (2 oz) caster sugar; 250 g (8 oz) plain flour, sifted; vanilla sugar, for sprinkling

Viennese Whirls

■ Place 16 mini silicone muffin cases on a baking sheet.

■ Beat together the butter and caster sugar until very pale and creamy. Beat in the flour and vanilla extract until smooth. Place in a piping bag fitted with a 1 cm (½ inch) star nozzle. Pipe a little mixture into the base of each case. Pipe a ring of the mixture on top to create nest shapes.

■ Bake in a preheated oven, 180°C (350°F), Gas Mark 4, for 15–20 minutes until pale golden. Leave in the cases for 5 minutes, then transfer to a wire rack. Impress holes into the centres of the nests if they have expanded during cooking. Leave to cool.

■ Place a little jam in the centre of each nest and sprinkle vanilla sugar over the edges.

MAKE THEM CHOCOLATEY

For chocolate thumbprint biscuits, make the biscuit mixture opposite, replacing 25 g (1 oz) of the flour with 25 g (1 oz) cocoa powder. Spoon the mixture into the cases and push a hole into the centre of each, using your thumb. Bake as opposite and leave to cool. Put 5 tablespoons chocolate hazelnut spread in a piping bag fitted with a small star nozzle and pipe a swirl into the centre of each.

MAKES 24

Preparation time 15 minutes
Cooking time 12 minutes

INGREDIENTS

1 10 cardamom pods

2 2 egg whites

3 ½ teaspoon hot chilli powder

4 75 g (3 oz) ground almonds

STORECUPBOARD

2 teaspoons cornflour; 125 g (4 oz) caster sugar

Chilli & Cardamom Morsels

■ Grease and line a large baking sheet with nonstick baking paper.

■ Crush the cardamom pods using a pestle and mortar to release the seeds. Remove the shells and crush the seeds until fairly finely ground.

■ Whisk the egg whites in a thoroughly clean bowl until peaking. Sift the cornflour and chilli powder into the bowl and sprinkle in the crushed cardamom. Add the sugar and ground almonds and gently fold the ingredients together to make a sticky paste.

■ Place in a piping bag fitted with a 1 cm (½ inch) plain nozzle and pipe fingers, 5 cm (2 inches) long, onto the baking sheet, spacing them slightly apart.

■ Bake in a preheated oven, 180°C (350°F), Gas Mark 4, for 10–12 minutes until crisp and pale golden. Transfer to a wire rack to cool.

A MILDER BISCUIT

For hazelnut & orange fingers, blend 75 g (3 oz) blanched hazelnuts in a food processor or blender until ground. Make the fingers opposite, omitting the spices and adding the finely grated rind of 1 small orange with the caster sugar and adding the hazelnuts instead of the ground almonds.

MAKES 16

Preparation time 15 minutes, plus soaking
Cooking time 12 minutes

INGREDIENTS

1 | 50 g (2 oz) raisins

2 | 4 tablespoons marsala

3 | 1 teaspoon instant espresso coffee powder, plus an extra ½ teaspoon

4 | 125 g (4 oz) natural yogurt

5 | 1 egg, beaten

STORECUPBOARD

2 teaspoons boiling water; 125 g (4 oz) self-raising flour; ½ teaspoon baking powder; 65 g (2½ oz) golden caster sugar; 2 tablespoons vegetable oil; 1½ teaspoons hot water; 40 g (1½ oz) icing sugar

Marsala Raisin Coffee Muffins

■ Put the raisins and marsala in a small saucepan and heat until hot but not boiling. Pour into a bowl and leave to stand for 2 hours until the raisins have plumped up.

■ Place 16 mini silicone muffin cases on a baking sheet.

■ Mix 1 teaspoon coffee powder with the boiling water. Sift the flour and baking powder into a bowl. Stir in the golden caster sugar.

■ Mix together the yogurt, egg, oil and coffee mixture and stir in the raisins and any unabsorbed liquid. Add to the dry ingredients. Using a large metal spoon, stir the ingredients together until only just combined. Divide among the cases.

■ Bake in a preheated oven, 200°C (400°F), Gas Mark 6, for about 12 minutes until risen and firm. Leave in the cases for 2 minutes, then transfer to a wire rack to cool.

■ Make the icing by mixing the remaining espresso coffee powder in a small bowl with the hot water until blended. Sift over the icing sugar, beat again, then drizzle over the muffins.

MAKE IT MOCHA

For mocha cream muffins, make the muffins opposite, omitting the raisins and marsala and replacing them with 50 g (2 oz) chopped white chocolate and 1 tablespoon cocoa powder. After baking, mix together 2 teaspoons caster sugar, ½ teaspoon ground cinnamon and ½ teaspoon cocoa powder and use to sprinkle generously over the muffins.

MAKES 24

Preparation time 20 minutes, plus standing
Cooking time 15 minutes

INGREDIENTS

1	butter, for greasing

2	65 g (2½ oz) ground almonds

3	2 egg whites

4	pink and green food colouring

STORECUPBOARD

50 g (2 oz) icing sugar; 100 g (3½ oz) caster sugar

French Macaroons

■ Grease and line 2 baking sheets with nonstick baking paper.

■ Put the icing sugar in a food processor with the ground almonds and blend to a very fine consistency.

■ Put the egg whites in a thoroughly clean bowl and whisk until stiffly peaking. Gradually whisk in the caster sugar, a tablespoonful at a time and whisking well after each addition, until thick and very glossy. Divide the mixture equally between 2 bowls and add a few drops of food colouring to each bowl. Divide the almond mixture equally between the 2 bowls and use a metal spoon to stir the mixtures gently to combine.

■ Place 1 colour in a piping bag fitted with a 1 cm (½ inch) plain nozzle and pipe 12 × 3 cm (1¼ inch) rounds onto 1 baking

sheet. Tap the baking sheet firmly to smooth the surfaces of the macaroons. Wash and dry the pipiing bag and piping nozzle and pipe 12 rounds in the second colour onto the other baking sheet. Leave to stand for 30 minutes.

■ Bake in a preheated oven, 160°C (325°F), Gas Mark 3, for about 15 minutes, or until the surfaces feel crisp. Leave to cool before carefully peeling away the paper.

Preparation time 25 minutes, plus cooling
Cooking time 12 minutes

INGREDIENTS

1	65 g (2½ oz) lightly salted butter, softened
2	1 egg
3	40 g (1½ oz) white chocolate, chopped into small pieces plus chocolate curls, to decorate
4	75 g (3 oz) raspberries
5	150 g (5 oz) medium-fat soft cheese

STORECUPBOARD

40 g (1½ oz) caster sugar; 65 g (2½ oz) self-raising flour; 1 tablespoon icing sugar

White Chocolate Raspberry Cupcakes

■ Place 16 mini silicone muffin cases on a baking sheet.

■ Put the butter, caster sugar, flour and egg in a bowl and beat with a hand-held electric whisk until light and creamy. Stir in the chopped chocolate and divide among the cases.

■ Bake in a preheated oven, 180°C (350°F), Gas Mark 4, for 10–12 minutes, or until risen and just firm. Leave in the cases for 2 minutes, then transfer to a wire rack to cool completely.

■ Make the topping by putting the raspberries in a bowl and crushing with a fork. Put the soft cheese and icing sugar in a separate bowl and beat until smooth. Stir the crushed raspberries into the mixture until lightly combined but not completely blended. Spoon over the tops of the cakes and decorate with the chocolate curls.

MAKES 24 SQUARES

Preparation time 25 minutes, plus cooling
Cooking time 55 minutes

INGREDIENTS

1 200 g (7 oz) lightly salted butter, softened, plus extra for greasing

2 225 g (7½ oz) stoned dates, chopped

3 150 ml (¼ pint) double cream

4 2 teaspoons vanilla bean paste

5 3 eggs

STORECUPBOARD

150 ml (¼ pint) water; 175 g (6 oz) light muscovado sugar; 100 g (3½ oz) caster sugar; 175 g (6 oz) self-raising flour; ½ teaspoon baking powder

Sticky Toffee & Date Squares

■ Grease and line a 28 × 18 cm (11 × 7 inch) shallow baking tin with nonstick baking paper. Put 125 g (4 oz) of the dates in a saucepan with the water and bring to the boil. Reduce the heat and cook gently for 5 minutes or until the dates are pulpy. Turn into a bowl and leave to cool. Put the cream, muscovado sugar and 75 g (3 oz) of the butter in a small saucepan and heat gently until the sugar dissolves. Bring to the boil and boil for 5 minutes or until thickened and caramelized. Leave to cool.

■ Put the remaining butter in a bowl with the caster sugar, vanilla bean paste and eggs, sift in the flour and baking powder and beat with a hand-held electric whisk until pale and creamy. Beat in the cooked dates and 100 ml (3½ fl oz) of the caramel mixture. Turn into the tin and level the surface. Scatter with the remaining dates.

■ Bake in a preheated oven, 180°C (350°F), Gas Mark 4, for 25 minutes, or until just firm. Spoon the remaining caramel on top and return to the oven for 15 minutes until the caramel has firmed. Transfer to a wire rack to cool.

TRY IT WITH CIDER-GLAZED APPLES

For cider-glazed apple slice, grease the tin as opposite. Put 175 g (6 oz) lightly salted softened butter, 175 g (6 oz) golden caster sugar, 200 g (7 oz) sifted self-raising flour, ½ teaspoon baking powder, 1 teaspoon ground mixed spice and 3 eggs in a bowl and beat with an electric hand whisk until smooth and creamy. Stir in 65 g (2½ oz) sultanas and spread in the tin. Core and slice 2 small red apples and scatter over the surface. Bake as opposite for 40 minutes or until just firm. Put 100 ml (3½ fl oz) cider in a saucepan and heat until reduced to about 1 tablespoon. Cool and mix with 75 g (3 oz) sifted golden icing sugar until smooth. Drizzle over the cake.

MAKES 16

Preparation time 20 minutes, plus cooling
Cooking time 12 minutes

INGREDIENTS

1   65 g (2½ oz) lightly salted butter, softened

2   1 egg

3   3 tablespoons limoncello liqueur

4   5 tablespoons lemon curd

5   75 g (3 oz) unsalted butter, softened

STORECUPBOARD

65 g (2½ oz) caster sugar; 65 g (2½ oz) self-raising
flour; finely grated rind of 1 lemon, plus
1 tablespoon of the juice; 50 g (2 oz) icing sugar,
plus extra for dusting

Lemon & Limoncello Cupcakes

■ Place 16 mini silicone muffin cases on
a baking sheet.

■ Put the salted butter, caster sugar, flour,
lemon rind and egg in a bowl and beat with
a hand-held electric whisk until light and
creamy. Divide among the cases.

■ Bake in a preheated oven, 180°C
(350°F), Gas Mark 4, for 10–12 minutes
until risen and just firm. Leave in the
cases for 2 minutes, then transfer to a
wire rack to cool. Drizzle 2 tablespoons
of the limoncello over the cakes and leave
to cool completely.

■ Reserve 2 tablespoons of the lemon
curd and spread the remainder over the
cakes with a palette knife.

■ Make the icing by putting the unsalted
butter, icing sugar, reserved limoncello,
reserved lemon curd and the lemon juice in
a bowl and beating well until smooth and
creamy. Place in a piping bag fitted with a
star nozzle and pipe swirls on top of each
cake. Serve lightly dusted with icing sugar.

TRY A DIFFERENT FRUIT

For rhubarb & orange cupcakes, make the sponge as opposite, using the finely grated rind of ½ orange instead of lemon. Divide among the cases. Cut 100 g (3½ oz) rhubarb into very thin diagonal slices and toss with 4 teaspoons caster sugar and a good pinch of ground ginger. Pile on top of the sponge bases and scatter with 2 tablespoons crushed flaked almonds. Bake as opposite and serve dusted with icing sugar.

MAKES 18

Preparation time 10 minutes
Cooking time 25 minutes

INGREDIENTS

| 1 | 150 g (5 oz) lightly salted butter, softened |

| 2 | 3 eggs |

| 3 | 1 teaspoon almond extract |

| 4 | 50 g (2 oz) chopped mixed nuts |

| 5 | 75 g (3 oz) mixed dried fruit |

STORECUPBOARD

150 g (5 oz) light muscovado sugar;
200 g (7 oz) self-raising flour

Fruit & Nut Cupcakes

■ Line 2 × 12-section bun tins with 18 paper cake cases. Put the butter, sugar, flour, eggs and almond extract in a bowl and beat with a hand-held electric whisk for 1–2 minutes until light and creamy.

■ Add the chopped nuts and dried fruit and stir until evenly combined. Divide the cake mixture between the paper cases.

■ Bake in a preheated oven, 180°C (350°F), Gas Mark 4, for 25 minutes until risen and just firm to the touch. Transfer to a wire rack to cool.

INDEX

almonds
almond brittle 110
almond praline cupcakes 90
French macaroons 180
fruited friands 44
pear and almond cake 60
Amaretti plum cakes 164
apples
blackberry and apple puffs 40
cider-glazed apple slices 185
chocolate apple pancakes 84
French apple flan 22
instant apple crumbles 142
steamed apple puddings 126
apricots
apricot clafouti 30
apricot tartlets 166
white chocolate and apricot blondies 78

baby butterflies 172
baked Alaska, mini 138
bananas
banoffee meringues 124
date and banana ripple slice 154
basil: tropical fruit and basil ice cream 28
berries
frozen berry yogurt ice cream 152
mini baked Alaska 138
tipsy berry waffles 38
biscuits
chilli and cardamom morsels 176
chocolate caramel shortbread 74
chocolate chip cookies 66
fairings 136
hazelnut and orange fingers 177
peanut butter cookies 140
strawberry and lavender shortcakes 116
blackberry and apple puffs 40
blackcurrant and mint soufflé 42

blondies, white chocolate and apricot 78
blueberries
blueberry tarts 158
peach and blueberry jalousie 50
tipsy berry waffles 38
Brazil nuts: chai teabread 104
breadcrumbs: instant apple crumbles 142
brittle, almond 110
brownies, rich chocolate 150
brûlée, nectarine 92

candied pistachio cake 94
caramel
caramel ice cream cake 98
chocolate caramel cake 99
chocolate caramel shortbread 74
warm pecan caramel cupcakes 170
caraway cake, orange and 128
cardamom: chilli and cardamom morsels 176
chai teabread 104
cherry crumble cake 32
chestnuts: sweet chestnut mess 106
chilli and cardamom morsels 176
chocolate 62–87
chocolate and raspberry soufflés 76
chocolate apple pancakes 84
chocolate caramel shortbread 74
chocolate chip cookies 66
chocolate chip teabread 72
chocolate ice cream 68
chocolate millefeuilles 108
chocolate puddle pudding 82
chocolate truffle cake 100
easy chocolate fudge cake 64
instant pear and chocolate crumble 142
minted white chocolate cakes 70

rich chocolate brownies 150
rocky road ice cream sundaes 122
sweet chestnut mess 106
white chocolate and apricot blondies 78
white chocolate and raspberry puffs 86
white chocolate coconut muffins 160
white chocolate raspberry cupcakes 182
churros 132
clafouti, apricot 30
coconut
coconut syllabub and almond brittle 110
white chocolate coconut muffins 160
coffee
marbled coffee cupcakes 118
Masala raisin coffee muffins 178
old-fashioned coffee cake 130
cookies
chocolate chip 66
peanut butter 140
cranberries
fruited friands 44
sweet cranberry and orange pie 56
white chocolate and apricot blondies 78
cream
banoffee meringues 124
chilled blackcurrant and mint soufflé 42
classic lemon tart 102
coconut syllabub and almond brittle 110
mini custard tarts 168
passion fruit cream cupcakes 162
passion fruit yogurt fool 112
strawberry and lavender shortcakes 116
strawberry macaroon cake 52

strawberry rosé jelly and syllabub 96
white chocolate and raspberry puffs 86
crème brûlée, nectarine 92
crumble, instant apple 142
crumble cakes, cherry 32
cupcakes
  almond praline 90
  Amaretti plum 164
  baby butterflies 172
  fruit and nut 188
  lemon and limoncello 186
  marbled coffee 118
  marshmallow cream cakes 182
  Masala raisin coffee 178
  mile-high marshmallow 80
  passion fruit cream 162
  warm pecan caramel 170
  white chocolate coconut 160
  white chocolate raspberry 182
custard tarts 168

dates
  date and banana ripple slice 154
  sticky toffee and date squares 184

elderflowers: gooseberry and elderflower pies 48

fairings 136
figs
  fig and honey pots 54
  iced fig slice 114
fool, passion fruit yogurt 112
French apple flan 22
French macaroons 180
friands, fruited 44
fruit
  fruit and nut cupcakes 188
  warm summer fruit trifle 144
  see also apples; cherries, etc
fudge
  banoffee meringues 124
  easy chocolate fudge cake 64

gooseberry and elderflower pies 48

honey: fig and honey pots 54

ice cream
  caramel ice cream cake 98
  chocolate 68
  frozen berry yogurt 152
  mini baked Alaska 138
  rocky road sundaes 122
  tropical fruit and basil 28

jalousie, peach and blueberry 50
jellies: strawberry rosé jelly and syllabub 96
  bucks fizz jelles 97

kaffir lime tart 24

lavender: strawberry and lavender shortcakes 116
lemons
  classic lemon tart 102
  lemon and limoncello cupcakes 186
  lemon and poppy seed cake 128
  lemon meringue pie 146
  lemon puddle pudding 34
limes: kaffir lime tart 24

macaroons
  French 180
  strawberry macaroon cake 52
mango and palm sugar tatin 46
marshmallows
  mile-high marshmallow cupcakes 80
  rocky road ice cream sundaes 122
Masala raisin coffee muffins 178
meringues
  banoffee 124
  lemon meringue pie 146
  mini baked Alaska 138
  raspberry ripple 148
  sweet chestnut mess 106

warm summer fruit trifle 144
mile-high marshmallow cupcakes 80
millefeuille, chocolate 108
mint
  chilled blackcurrant and mint soufflé 42
  minted white chocolate cakes 70
muffins
  Masala raisin coffee 178
  white chocolate coconut 160

nectarine brûlée 92
nuts: fruit and nut cupcakes 188
  see also almonds; pecans, etc

oranges
  orange and caraway cake 128
  rhubarb slumps 26
  sweet cranberry and orange pie 56

pancakes, chocolate apple 84
  peach melba 85
  sweet chestnut 107
passion fruit
  passion fruit cream cupcakes 162
  passion fruit yogurt fool 112
peaches
  peach and blueberry jalousie 50
  peach melba pie 134
peanut butter cookies 140
pears
  instant pear and chocolate crumble 142
  pear and almond cake 60
pecan nuts: warm pecan caramel cupcakes 170
pies
  gooseberry and elderflower 48
  peach melba 134
  sweet cranberry and orange 56

pistachio nuts: candied pistachio cake 94
plums: Amaretti plum cakes 164
poppy seeds: lemon and poppy seed cake 128
praline: almond praline cupcakes 90
puddle puddings
chocolate 82
lemon 34
puffs
blackberry and apple 40
white chocolate and raspberry 86

raisins: Masala raisin coffee muffins 178
raspberries
chocolate and raspberry soufflés 76
instant raspberry sorbet 58
peach melba pie 134
raspberry ripple meringues 148
tipsy berry waffles 38
white chocolate and raspberry puffs 86
white chocolate raspberry cupcakes 182
redcurrants: peach and redcurrant cupcakes 163
rhubarb slumps 26

rocky road ice cream sundaes 122
rosé wine: strawberry rosé jelly and syllabub 96

shortbread, chocolate caramel 74
shortcakes, strawberry and lavender 116
sorbet, instant raspberry 58
soufflés
chilled blackcurrant and mint 42
chocolate and raspberry 76
strawberries
strawberry and lavender shortcakes 116
strawberry macaroon cake 52
strawberry rosé jelly and syllabub 96
sultanas: sticky sultana and bran slice 36
summer fruit trifle 144
sundaes
frozen berry yogurt 152
rocky road ice cream 122
syllabub
coconut 110
strawberry rosé 96

tarts
apricot 166
blueberry 158
classic lemon 102
custard 168
French apple flan 22
kaffir lime 24
lemon meringue pie 146
mango and palm sugar tatin 46
peach and blueberry jalousie 50
teabreads
chai 104
chocolate chip 72
tipsy berry waffles 38
toffee
banoffee meringues 124
sticky toffee and date squares 184
trifle, summer fruit 144
tropical fruit and basil ice cream 28

Viennese whirls 174

waffles, tipsy berry 38

yogurt
frozen berry yogurt ice cream 152
passion fruit yogurt fool 112

PICTURE CREDITS

Photography copyright © Octopus Publishing Group / Stephen Conroy 7, 9, 27, 49, 57, 61, 65, 67, 69, 107, 109, 113, 135, 145, 159, 161, 167; Will Heap 5, 20–21, 29, 31, 35, 41, 51, 59, 83, 85, 97, 123, 127, 139, 143, 147, 153, 156-157, 165, 173, 175, 177, 179, 181, 183, 185, 187; Neil Mersh 39, 55, 111; David Munns 71, 81, 91, 119, 163, 171; Emma Neish 62–63, 75; Lis Parsons 43, 77, 103; Gareth Sambidge 189; William Shaw 6, 8, 33, 37, 45, 53, 73, 79, 88-89, 95, 101, 105, 115, 117, 120–121, 125, 129, 131, 133, 137, 149, 151, 155, 169; Simon Smith 93; Ian Wallace 23, 25, 47, 87, 99, 141.